Round Hall Nutshells

Land Law

AUSTRALIA

LBC Information Services
Sydney

CANADA AND THE USA

Carswell
Toronto

NEW ZEALAND

Brooker's
Wellington

SINGAPORE AND MALAYSIA

Thomson Information (S.E. Asia)
Singapore

Round Hall Nutshells

Land Law

Ruth Cannon
LLB, B.C.L. (Oxon), B.L.

SERIES EDITOR

Bruce Carolan

DUBLIN
ROUND HALL SWEET & MAXWELL
2001

Published in 2001 by
Round Hall Ltd
43 Fitzwilliam Place
Dublin 2

Typeset by
Round Hall Ltd, Dublin

Printed by
ColourBooks, Dublin

ISBN 1-85800-170-6

A catalogue record for this book
is available from the British Library.

Table of Contents

Table of Cases

Table of Legislation

Chapter 1

Introduction to Land Law and Equity

There are a number of purposes behind this book. The first is to provide the beginner in land law with an outline knowledge of the subject. Secondly, the book aims to assist the student who has covered a number of topics in land law quite well, but is uncertain how these topics fit into the general structure of the subject. The third purpose of the book is to help those who are preparing for exams and are under pressure to cover the important material quickly.

This introductory chapter begins by giving an outline of a typical Irish land law course. It then discusses the various sources of land law.

There are three main sources of land law: the common law, equity and statute law. Students often find it difficult to understand the way in which these diverse sources interact with one another. In particular, comprehension of the role played by the courts of equity may be problematic. Evidence of the huge impact equity has had on land law is to be found throughout the course. For this reason the role of equity in land law is also summarised in this introductory chapter.

I: OUTLINE OF IRISH LAND LAW

The standard Irish land law course has two main components:

- It outlines the various types of rights which people may have in relation to land.
- It also deals to some extent with the ways in which these rights may be acquired.

Interests in land

Lawyers normally refer to rights over land as *interests in land*. There are a number of different interests in land (see below, Chapters 2–10).

1

Freehold ownership

First of all, we need to discuss what is meant by ownership of land. Ownership is generally understood by the non-lawyer to be the right to permanent exclusive possession of land, the owner having the right to dispose of it to whoever he wishes, either during his lifetime or by will. In practice, matters are not so simple, since land law recognises different types of ownership. The above situation describes the fee simple freehold owner.

Generally speaking, a freehold owner is someone who has the exclusive right to possession of land with no landlord above him. However, not all freehold owners have the right to exclusive possession of the land forever. There are other freehold owners, such as the holder of a fee tail or life estate, whose freehold interest determines on their death. These individuals do not have the right to freely transfer the land, nor may they leave it by will.

Leasehold ownership

In addition, a tenant under a lease is also described by land law as the owner of land. Although he is not the freehold owner, he has what is known as leasehold ownership, *i.e.* the right to exclusive possession of the land according to the terms of his agreement with the landlord.

Licensees

In contrast to leasehold ownership, a licence over land is a mere permission from the owner of land to occupy it There is no agreement between the owner (licensor) and occupier (licensee) to hold as landlord and tenant. Licensees have lesser rights than tenants. Some licensees have given consideration and they are in a stronger position. Nonetheless, a licence is merely a personal right and this creates problems for the licensee when the owner of the land over which the licence subsists sells on the land to a third party. The third party is entitled to throw the licensee off the land.

Easements

The term "easement" is used to describe a limited right to carry out a particular act on a neighbour's land or, in some cases, to prevent him from doing a particular act on his land. Easements may be positive or negative. An example of a positive easement would be a right to cross a defined path on a neighbour's land to get to a main road. A right, held by a landowner, to stop a neighbour building on his own land, on the ground that it reduces the level of light coming through the windows of the landowner's house, constitutes a negative easement.

Freehold Covenants

Additionally, the device of freehold covenants gives a limited right of control over one's neighbour by requiring him to do or, more usually, refrain from doing a particular act. A may enter into a covenant with B whereby B promises not to build on B's land. A has the benefit of the covenant, namely the right to sue if B breaches his promise. Moreover, future owners of A's land may be able to enforce the covenant against future owners of B's land.

Interests in land can be divided into possessory and non-possessory interests. Some interests in land, such as freehold ownership, leasehold ownership and some licences, give the holder the right to possession of land.

Other interests, such as easements and covenants, do not give the holder the right to possession of the land over which they exist but allow him either to carry out certain limited functions on the land or to control the use of it by its occupier in some way.

Acquiring interests in land

Freehold ownership of land may be transferred *inter vivos* or on death. A transfer *inter vivos* is a transfer from someone who is still alive at the time of the transfer. *Inter vivos* transfers may be either sales or voluntary conveyances, namely gifts. Often ownership of land is transferred *inter vivos* in return for a loan of money, with a condition that title to the land will be returned to the borrower once the money is repaid. This is known as a mortgage. Mortgages are subject to special rules and are dealt with later in this book (see Chapter 13: Mortgages).

Transfer on death may occur by will or, if there is no valid will, according to the rules of intestacy, and is regulated by the Succession Act 1965.

The rules for creation and transfer of leases, easements, and rights under covenants are dealt with in the chapters on these topics.

De facto ownership of land may also be acquired by adverse possession of the land for 12 years.

II: EQUITY

Having briefly summarised the topics covered in this text, it is now proposed to consider the important historical concept of equity and the role it plays in our modern land law system. Equity's influence on land law has been immense.

What is "equity"?

The term "equity" is used to refer to the legal rules and concepts developed by the courts of chancery as opposed to the common law courts.

The original basis for our land law is the common law, as developed by the common law courts. However, in the late Middle Ages the rival courts of equity/chancery were developed. They introduced changes in the law, modifying the common law to some extent. Because the courts of equity co-existed with the common law courts, there was initial rivalry between the two courts. This culminated in an attempt by the common law courts to deny the validity of the rules of equity. However, the seventeenth-century political situation led to the courts of equity being assigned superiority over those of the common law. Thereafter the common law courts could not nullify the modifications introduced by equity.

There remained, however, some procedural difficulties for the litigant who wished to rely on equitable rules. To invoke a common law principle, it was necessary to apply to the common law courts, whereas those who wished to rely on an equitable rule had to go to the courts of equity. This led to expense and delay in litigation. This was remedied by the Supreme Court of Judicature (Ireland) Act 1877. The position today is that a single court, the High Court, has the responsibility of administering the rules of the common law, subject to the modifications introduced by equity and statute law.

Reform of mortgages

Equity intervened to modify the harsh common law rules relating to mortgages (see Chapter 13: Mortgages).

Equitable interests

The most important change introduced by equity was the development of equitable interests. These were interests in land which were not regarded as valid by the common law courts, but which equity felt should be recognised. They are to be contrasted with legal interests, namely rights which were recognised and enforced at common law.

Equitable interests are interests which were not regarded as valid rights under the old common law rules but are valid according to the doctrines of equity.

They include:

- The interest of a beneficiary under a trust (see Chapter 3: Equitable Ownership and the Statute of Uses).
- The right to sue under a restrictive covenant (see Chapter 10: Freehold Covenants).
- The right to claim an interest in land under the equitable doctrine of estoppel (see Chapter 8: Licences and Estoppel).
- Certain mortgages and leases which do not satisfy the common law formalities for the creation of such interests, but which equity feels should be recognised nonetheless (see Chapter 7: Leasehold Ownership, and Chapter 13: Mortgages).

It is still important to distinguish between legal and equitable interests today. Equitable interests are weaker than legal interests in one respect. They will be extinguished if unregistered land over which they exist comes into the hands of a purchaser of the legal estate for value without notice. (For a definition of this privileged person, who is commonly known as *equity's darling*, see Chapter 11: Transfer of Land). Equity feels that it would be unjust for such an individual to be bound by equitable interests.

The common law does not accord any favours to such a person and legal proprietary interests will bind everyone who purchases or obtains unregistered land over which they subsist.

Mere equities

Finally, equity recognises rights to set aside a transaction for undue influence, mistake or misrepresentation in situations where the common law does not. We call these particular rights mere equities because they are not as strong in nature as equitable interests such as equitable ownership, restrictive covenant rights, estoppel rights and the equitable leases and mortgages mentioned above.

Chapter 2

Freehold Ownership

I: TYPES OF FREEHOLD OWNERSHIP

There are four types of freehold ownership, known as the four freehold estates:

- The fee simple.
- The fee tail.
- The life estate.
- The estate *pur autre vie*.

The fee simple

The first and most powerful form of freehold ownership is the fee simple. The word "fee" is a reference to "forever". The added word "simple" means "without qualification". The owner of a standard fee simple estate has the right to ownership of the relevant land forever. He is the absolute owner of the land.

However, quite apart from the standard fee simple estate, there are two modified fee simple estates which are not quite equivalent to absolute ownership. These are the determinable fee simple and the fee simple subject to a condition.

The determinable fee simple is a fee simple estate which will end automatically on the happening of a specified event, which might or might not happen. Hence, although the estate might not go on forever, it is described as a fee simple, albeit a modified one, because it has the potential to go on for ever if the event in question does not occur. If the event occurs the estate will revert back automatically to the person who granted the determinable fee. His interest is known as a possibility of reverter. Alternatively, the grantor may provide in the original grant that the fee simple will go to someone else if the event occurs. This is known as a gift over after a determinable fee.

The second type of modified fee simple is the fee simple upon a condition, which has also been called a conditional fee simple. Again, this may come to an end if the specified condition or event occurs and the grantor or the person specified to get the fee simple on occurrence of the condition exercises the right of entry onto the property. The distinction between a conditional and a determinable fee is that with a conditional fee the mere happening of the event will not automatically cause the estate to end. It merely gives the grantor or the holder of the gift over a right of entry and the estate only terminates on the exercise of this right.

When faced with a grant of a modified fee simple, in order to decide whether it is a conditional or determinable fee, it is necessary to look at the words used in the grant. Certain words are regarded as giving rise to a determinable fee simple and others are regarded as giving rise to a conditional fee simple.

Words such as "while", "during", "as long as" and "until", if included in the grant of a modified fee, signify a determinable fee simple. Conversely, words such as "on condition that", "provided that" and "but if" create a fee simple upon a condition.

Sometimes there may be an attempted grant of a modified fee which may fail because the imposition of the condition or determining event is inconsistent with the nature of a fee simple or contrary to public policy or constitutional principles.

If the grant is one of a determinable fee and the imposition of the determining event is objectionable the whole gift fails. The grantee gets nothing. However, if the condition in a conditional fee is impermissible the condition will be severed from the rest of the grant and struck down, the result being that the grantee obtains an absolute fee simple. This is another important difference between determinable fee simples and fee simples upon a condition.

The following is a list of potentially impermissible restrictions on modified fees:

- restrictions on alienation;
- restrictions on residence;
- name and arms clauses;
- restrictions on marriage;
- ethnic, sectarian and religious restrictions;

The fee tail

A fee tail is the second type of freehold estate recognised. It is a lesser estate than the fee simple because it does not confer absolute ownership. Instead, it is what is known as an estate of inheritance. If land is given to Georgina in fee tail, this means that she will have the use of the land for her life but on her death it will automatically pass to her descendants according to the rules of primogeniture. On her death it will transfer to her eldest son, and if she has no sons, it will be divided among her daughters according to the rules of coparcenary.

The same process will be repeated in the next generation. Thus, when Georgina dies and her eldest son inherits the land, he too will merely get a life estate in the land and his eldest son will inherit, etc. If he has no children then it is necessary to go back to the previous generation and pass the land to Georgina's second son, if he is alive, or his descendants, if he is not.

The significance of the fee tail is that it creates a succession of life estates which go on forever according to the rules of primogeniture. The fee tail will only end if all Georgina's blood descendants die out.

In the meantime the land subject to the fee tail is completely inalienable. All that any individual who takes under the fee tail may sell is their life estate in the land. This means that a purchaser from that person will merely get an estate *pur autre vie*, *i.e.* an estate lasting until the death of the person currently entitled under the fee tail. This is a very uncertain interest and it is not surprising that land subject to a fee tail is virtually impossible to alienate.

As regards the historical origins of the fee tail, conveyancers had been trying for years to keep land in the family through a device known as the maritagium. However, they found their intentions continually circumvented by the courts. The result was the passing of the statute *De Donis Conditionalibus* 1285, which expressly permitted the fee tail described above, seeing it as an appropriate mechanism of keeping land in the family.

As centuries passed, the problems of the fee tail became all too apparent. It tied up land in such a way as to make estate owners impoverished and incapable of financially adapting to the changes of the agricultural and industrial revolutions. The result was that many estates fell into disrepair and remained that way. As already stated, it was impossible to alienate land subject to a fee tail.

Astute conveyancers developed a number of devices for "barring fee tails" and granting the person then in possession under the fee tail (the *tenant in tail*) a fee simple instead. However, the Fines and Recoveries Act 1834 represented a milestone, since it laid down a relatively simple and clearly defined mechanism for converting a fee tail into a fee simple.

A present or future tenant in tail may achieve this result by executing a disentailing assurance and enrolling it in the Central Office of the High Court within six months of its execution. A tenant in tail with possibility of issue extinct is not allowed to avail of this mechanism. The one drawback is that the tenant in tail has to get the consent of an individual known as the protector of the settlement, if such person exists. The individual currently in possession of the land under the settlement (the present tenant in tail) qualifies as a protector of the settlement. This only presents a problem when the person seeking to execute the disentailing assurance is a future tenant in tail. Alternatively, the document creating the fee tail might have nominated a particular person as the protector of the settlement.

If the tenant in tail fails to get the consent of the protector of the settlement, he is left with a base fee. A base fee extinguishes the claims of the descendants of the tenant in tail, but does not extinguish the claims of those who have the reversion should the descendants of the tenant in tail ever die out. A base fee may be remedied by the tenant in tail or his descendants executing a fresh disentailing assurance properly. If the land has been transferred to a third party who was not entitled under the entail, he may alternatively be able to bar the claims of the reversioners or remaindermen by buying out their interests. Alternatively, he may avail of section 19 of the Statute of Limitations which provides that possession by the third party for 12 years after the determination of the protectorship will bar the reversioners/remaindermen.

If the tenant in tail makes an even greater mistake and fails to enrol the disentailing assurance in the High Court in time, then he is left with a lesser interest still, a voidable base fee. Not only does this estate not bar the claims of remaindermen, but it also allows the issue in tail to enter on the land at any time and revive the fee tail. However, under section 19, 12 years' possession after determination of the protectorship operates to bar the claims of the issue as well as the remaindermen and reversioners.

So far we have been talking about the fee tail general. However, there are also specialised types of fee tail which can be created. It is not uncommon to find a fee tail under which only descendants of one particular gender can inherit. This would be a fee tail male or a fee tail female. Alternatively, there may be a fee tail under which only descendants of a particular couple, as opposed to a particular person, can inherit. For example, a settlement made at the time of the marriage of Eileen and Patrick may restrict the descendants to benefit to descendants of both Eileen and Patrick "to Patrick and the heirs of his body begotten upon Eileen".

Specialised fee tails can be barred under the Fines and Recoveries Act 1834 in exactly the same way as general fee tails.

The life estate/estate *pur autre vie*

The owner of a life estate only has an estate in the land for his life. All that he is able to sell to another is an estate *pur autre vie* which is an estate for the life of another person, in this case the life of himself, the vendor.

The owner of an estate *pur autre vie* is in the same position as the holder of a life estate, only weaker. The continuance of his estate is dependent on the continuance of the life of another person. This is a most uncertain interest and is impossible to alienate.

Both owners are subject to the doctrine of waste. This means that they are not allowed to damage the property in such a way as to reduce the value of the property to the people who come after them, and if they do, either they or their estate will have to pay compensation.

II: WORDS OF LIMITATION

Transferring a fee simple

It is essential to understand the concept of words of limitation when dealing with freehold estates, particularly fee simple estates. When an individual buys or receives a gift of a fee simple estate *inter vivos*, it is very important that certain phrases should be used in the document transferring the property. If these phrases are not included, the transferee may end up with only a life estate.

To obtain a fee simple from someone during their life (rather than on death) it is normally necessary to:

- buy from someone who *has* a fee simple (as we know, if the vendor has a fee tail/life estate, all that can be transferred is an estate *pur autre vie*);

- *include* one of the following forms of words in the conveyance:

> "to [the transferee] and his heirs"; or
> "to [the transferee] in fee simple".

These exact forms of words must be used. Even if an intention to convey a fee simple is clear, if the precise words are not used the transferee will only receive a life estate. Conversely, once the right formula is down in full, the fact that superfluous words have been added after it will not stop a fee simple from passing.

However, under section 7 of the Conveyancing Act 1881, a transferee who ends up with a life estate because of incorrect words of limitation may compel the vendor to re-execute the conveyance using the proper words of limitation. But this provision only applies if the transferee has given consideration.

There are situations, however, in which the fee simple may be transferred without the need for any words of limitation. No words of limitation are necessary for a transfer of registered land. In addition, if property is left by will, the beneficiary will get a fee simple without the need for any words of limitation being used in the will, so long as it is clear that the testator intended him to have the property absolutely. Finally, if a fee simple is being transferred *inter vivos* to a company there is no need for words of limitation since a company, not being a natural person, cannot hold a life estate.

Creating a fee tail or life estate

It is not possible for the holder of a fee tail or a life estate to transfer an equivalent estate, but these estates may be created by a fee simple owner of the land and there are particular words that he must use to do so.

To create a fee tail *inter vivos* or by will, it is necessary to use one of the following three formulae:

> "to X and the heirs of his flesh";
> "to X and the heirs of his body"; or
> "to X in tail".

If these words are omitted the result will be a transfer of a life estate if the conveyance is *inter vivos* and a transfer of a fee simple if the gift is contained in a will.

A testator who wants to create a life estate in his will must make this very clear. There is a presumption that if property is transferred by will, the testator intended to transfer the fee simple in the property. However, as we have seen, it is easy to create a life estate *inter vivos*. This may be done merely by omitting to use any words of limitation at all.

The rule in *Shelley's Case*

The final matter in relation to words of limitation is the rule in *Shelley's Case* ((1581) 1 Co.Rep.88b). This rule arises in a situation where there is a gift "to Mary, remainder to her heirs". This was used as a way of keeping land in the family. On first appearances, Mary only had a life estate and could not sell the land.

The courts soon intervened to prevent this and treated "heirs" as a word of limitation giving Mary the fee simple. The rule may be summarised as follows:

> When an estate in freehold is given to a person, and by the same disposition that estate is limited to his heirs or the heirs of his body, they are words of limitation and not words of purchase.

The words "remainder to" are ignored and the transfer is read as if it were "to Mary and her heirs".

III: HYBRID INTERESTS

Freehold ownership may be distinguished from leasehold ownership, which will be considered in Chapter 7. Leasehold ownership is the right to possession of land subject to a lease. A lease is an agreement between the freehold owner and the occupier which is intended to create a landlord and tenant relationship. The occupier under a lease is described as the leasehold owner. Leasehold ownership imposes certain obligations on the tenant such as the duty to pay rent. It is also regulated by statute.

Normally a landlord has a reversion; the leasehold ownership will not last forever, and when the period specified for the lease comes to an end the landlord will get his property back absolutely. However, there are some situations where a lease does last for ever and these fall into the category of property interests known as hybrid interests.

Hybrid interests have both freehold and leasehold characteristics. Their freehold tendencies are evident from looking at their duration. They either last forever, akin to a fee simple, or they are determined by the length of someone's life, in a similar fashion to a life estate.

However, they have certain characteristics more appropriate to leases, in particular the fact of periodic payments to an overlord. None of the freehold estates mentioned above involve the making of such payments.

These hybrid interests fall into two categories:

- leases for lives; and
- fee farm grants.

Leases for lives

Leases for lives are leases whose length is determined by the lives of one or more persons. Thus, the duration of such "leases" is determined in a manner more suitable to a freehold than a leasehold estate.

However, their description as "leases" is not inappropriate either because they have leasehold characteristics such as a requirement to pay rent and to observe any covenants in the lease.

Fee farm grants

Fee farm grants arise where there exists a fee simple estate with some leasehold characteristics, such as the holder of the fee simple being under a perpetual obligation to pay a rent to the grantor. There are three forms of fee farm grant:

- Fee farm grants which arise from subinfeudation *non obstante Quia Emptores*. As students may know from studying the medieval concept of tenure, the statute *Quia Emptores* 1290 prohibited new grants of land which created a lord/tenant relationship. After *Quia Emptores*, the only person entitled to make such new grants was the King. In some cases in Ireland, the King granted tenure to certain individuals and also purported to exempt them from *Quia Emptores* and to give them permission to create new lord/tenant relationships. The result is that some property in Ireland is held under the old medieval tenure system. The holders of the land hold it as tenants under the feudal system. That is to say, they have a fee simple estate in the land but are required to pay a rent to the descendants of the grantor who are in the position of their lords.

- Fee farm grants which arise under the Renewable Leasehold Conversion Act 1849. This Act allowed perpetually renewable leases, such as leaseholds for lives renewable for ever, to be converted into fee simple. A fee farm rent is still payable to the landlord and he can forfeit for non-payment of rent or for breach of covenant.

  The Landlord and Tenant (Amendment) Act 1980 provides that perpetually renewable leases which had not been converted under the 1849 Act were to be regarded as held in fee simple from 1980 onwards. Since the 1980 Act does not use the word "fee farm grant" it is uncertain whether the tenant still has an obligation to pay rent.

- Fee farm grants which arise under Deasy's Act. Deasy's Act 1860 remains one of the leading pieces of landlord and tenant legislation in Ireland. However, it blurred the distinction between leasehold and freehold ownership somewhat by providing that a reversion on the part of the landlord was not necessary for a valid lease to exist. All that was necessary was an agreement between the parties to hold as landlord and tenant, combined with the payment of rent. Thus, it is possible to have leases created under Deasy's Act which last forever, but have all the ordinary incidents of the landlord/tenant relationship.

Chapter 3

Equitable Ownership and the Statute of Uses

I: THE TRUST

The development of equity and its rules has already been discussed (see Chapter 1: Introduction to Land Law and Equity). It was mentioned that equity developed a doctrine known as the trust whereby one person held the legal title to land for the benefit of another. The medieval device of the use laid the foundation for the modern legal concept of the trust.

Like the medieval use, the trust is a mechanism whereby one individual known as a trustee holds the legal title to land not for his own benefit, but for the benefit of another individual known as a beneficiary. The trustee cannot profit from his dealings with the trust property, even though he is the legal owner of it.

Only the beneficiary is allowed to take a substantive benefit from the trust property. In practical terms he is the real owner of it, even though he is not the owner at common law. However, the bundle of rights conferred by equity on a beneficiary under a trust are so great that he is described as the equitable owner of the property. In some cases the equitable rights of the beneficiary may even extend to compelling the trustee to transfer the legal title to the property over to him.

Describing someone as being the equitable owner of property or as owning an equitable estate in property means the same thing. Basically, these terms refer to the fact that the legal owner of the property in question holds it on trust for that person, and is not allowed to draw a benefit from it for himself.

The creation of a trust separates the legal and equitable estates in the property. The trustee, as the legal owner, has common law rights over the property but equity requires him to exercise his common law

15

rights for the benefit of the beneficiary, who is therefore known as the equitable owner.

In contrast, if no trust exists in relation to property, the common law owner is the absolute owner and is not curtailed by equity from exercising his common law rights.

A trust of property can be created either expressly or impliedly.

Express trusts

An express trust is created either when the owner of property expressly declares himself trustee of it for the benefit of someone else or, alternatively, when he conveys it to a third party to hold as trustee for the benefit of that person. In other words, an express trust is one which is intentionally created by the grantor of the land. Sometimes express trusts are created for tax avoidance purposes, or because the beneficiary under the trust is a minor and incapable of managing the gift, or perhaps because the settlor is afraid that the beneficiary will dissipate the property if given the absolute interest in it.

Implied trusts

There are also a number of situations where trusts will be implied by the courts. For example, if an individual buys property in someone else's name, or makes a gift of his property to another person, equity presumes a resulting trust in his favour. He is presumed not to intend to give his property away without receiving a benefit in return.

What happens in this situation is that the legal ownership in the property passes to the recipient of the gift, who is regarded as holding the gift on trust for the person making the gift. This kind of implied trust is known as a resulting trust because the gift effectively results back to the grantor. The presumption of resulting trust can be rebutted by evidence of an intention on the part of the grantor that the recipient should have absolute title to the property.

Equity also implies constructive trusts in a number of miscellaneous situations in order to meet the demands of justice.

II: THE STATUTE OF USES

It is now proposed to examine the historical development of the trust and its predecessor the use. The most important fact to remember about the use is that it was the historical forerunner of the trust.

However, the mechanism of the use also caused many other changes in land law and conveyancing generally, and some of them will be mentioned here.

As stated above, the medieval concept of a use was very similar to that of a trust. It involved the legal owner of land holding it "to the use of" (for the benefit of) someone else.

When land was conveyed to A to be held "to the use of" B, equity began to enforce the use and treated A as bound to give any benefit from the land to B. In this way there arose a separation of legal and equitable ownership. A was the legal owner of the land, but equity treated B as the real owner of the land for all practical purposes. A was known as the *feoffee to uses* and B was known as the *cestui que use*. Today we would describe A as the trustee and B as the beneficiary.

Creating a separation of legal and equitable ownership in this way was highly convenient. Legal ownership in the Middle Ages was very much curtailed by feudal rules relating to tenure. The common law required the legal owner to pay dues known as reliefs when he inherited the land. If he was a child when he inherited, the lord had the right to take his land and administer it until he came of age.

In addition, the common law refused to allow an owner of land to dispose of his property by will. It could only pass on his death according to the rules of primogeniture. Furthermore, at common law a person could not convey land to himself, which he might wish to do in order to create a form of co-ownership between himself and another person, such as his spouse.

The mechanism of the use allowed all these common law restrictions to be avoided:

- It allowed an individual to convey his property by will.
- It allowed an individual to convey his property to himself.
- It allowed an individual to avoid feudal dues such as reliefs and wardship. These were incidents which arose on the death of a tenant. By conveying his land to a younger friend as he grew older to hold for his own use for his life and for the use of his heirs after his death, a tenant could take steps to make sure that his heirs would not be subject to these incidents on his death. The reason for this lay in the fact that the feudal dues arose at common law, which did not recognise a beneficiary under a use as having any rights in relation to the land and so did not regard him as liable to pay reliefs, etc. Nonetheless, equity would

enforce the rights of the tenant's heirs in the land after his death, so in effect they succeeded to the land without having to pay the customary charge.

- It allowed new future interests to be created which were not limited by the common law remainder rules (see Chapter 4: Future Interests).

In effect, the use was being employed to avoid the harshness of the feudal tenure system. However, it necessarily held disadvantages for those who were lords under the tenure system. By and large this was not a problem at the lower levels of the system, where the lords were themselves tenants to higher lords and so could benefit from the use themselves in their capacity as tenants. But at the top of the feudal pyramid was the King, who was nobody's tenant. Those at the top of the pyramid, particularly the Crown, saw evidence of a reduction in their feudal dues, and viewed the use as a serious problem. The net result was the passing of the Statute of Uses 1535. This Act was adopted in Ireland in 1634. It still remains in force today.

The Statute of Uses was designed to stop individuals avoiding their feudal obligations by way of the use. It achieved this not by abolishing the use, but by executing it. The Statute provided that wherever land was held by one person to the use of someone else, the *cestui que use* or beneficiary should get the legal estate in the land. The *feoffee to uses* dropped out of the picture and there was no longer a separation of legal and beneficial ownership. The legal and equitable estates merged in the *cestui que use* who became the absolute owner of the land.

Example 1: to Peter and his heirs to the use of Niall and his heirs

Prior to the Statute of Uses Peter was treated as the owner of the land at common law. However, equity was prepared to compel Peter to hold the land not for his own benefit, but for the benefit of Niall. Niall was the only person equity regarded as capable of taking a benefit from the land. In this transaction, Peter was the *feoffee to uses* and Niall was the *cestui que use*.

After the Statute of Uses came into force, Peter dropped out of the picture. The use in favour of Niall was executed so as to give Niall not only the equitable, but also the legal estate. Niall was now the legal owner of the land again.

It is worth noting that the Statute did not execute uses of leasehold land, nor active uses (uses where the *feoffee to uses* had active duties to perform). Neither did it execute uses where the *feoffee to uses* was a corporation.

In Ireland, the Statute of Wills was passed at the same time as the Statute of Uses. It allowed individuals to convey property by will. Therefore, one function of the use was no longer necessary.

One benefit of the Statute of Uses was that it now meant that individuals could convey property to themselves even more effectively. Previously they had only been able to convey the equitable estate. Now, because of the Statute of Uses, they were able to convey absolute ownership. This facilitated the development of co-ownership.

Another, more dubious, advantage of the Statute of Uses was that it encouraged the development of future interests. By executing uses containing remainders, the statute allowed the development of a new kind of future interest, the legal executory interest, which did not have to comply with the common law remainder rules (see Chapter 4: Future Interests).

The main disadvantage of the Statute of Uses was that tenants were unable to avoid paying their feudal dues. However, this disadvantage became less and less significant over the years as the feudal system disintegrated.

With the decline of the feudal system, however, came a decision on the part of the Court of Chancery to circumvent the Statute of Uses in one regard and reintroduce the facility of separate legal and equitable ownership. They did this by developing the concept of a double use, alternatively known as the use upon a use.

Example 2: to B to the use of C to the use of D
In *Sambach v. Dalston* ((1634) Tothill 188) the Court of Chancery held that only the first use was executed by the Statute of Uses, so as to give C the legal ownership. The second use was not executed by the statute, and vested the equitable ownership in D. The net result was that C was the legal owner and D the equitable owner. The operation of the Statute of Uses could be avoided by inserting an extra use in a conveyance.

Example 3: to Simon and his heirs to the use of Peter and his heirs to the use of Niall and his heirs
In example 1 "to Peter and his heirs to the use of Niall and his heirs", we saw that after the enactment of the Statute Niall ended up back where he started, the reluctant holder of the legal estate in the prop-

erty. However, after *Sambach v. Dalston,* the grantor's original aim could be achieved if the conveyance were altered by inserting an extra use at the very beginning. Here the grantor's original intention is achieved. The first use is executed and Simon drops out of the picture. Peter is the legal owner under the Statute of Uses. However, he is not the equitable owner because equity regards the second use in favour of Niall as creating equitable ownership only, refusing to treat it as executed under the Statute.

It may be asked whether the above judicial policy was not in flagrant breach of the statute. Certainly, it was a fairly blatant circumvention of legislation. The reason that the judges were allowed to get away with this tactic was that, by the time of *Sambach v. Dalston,* the concerns which had prompted the enactment of the Statute of Uses no longer carried weight. The purpose of the statute was to counter the avoidance of feudal dues; two hundred years later, the feudal system had broken down and feudal dues were no longer an important issue.

The double use soon began to be written in an abbreviated form. First, it was cut down *"to A to the use of A to the use of B",* and then shortened further *"unto and to the use of A in trust for B".*

Example 4: unto and to the use of Peter and his heirs in trust for Niall and his heirs

This is the wording used today to create an express trust. If the five words *"and to the use of"* are forgotten, the conveyance passes absolute ownership, rather than merely the equitable ownership, to Niall.

So to this extent the Statute of Uses still retains significant importance for conveyancers. It regulates the wording they must use in a conveyance. If they are creating a trust and they forget to insert the second use then they may be susceptible to a legal action for negligence.

Chapter 4

Future Interests

I: INTRODUCTION

Future interests are interests which do not give rise to ownership rights at the present date in time, but which may give ownership rights at some future date. A knowledge of equitable ownership and the Statute of Uses (see Chapter 3) is vital in order to understand the law on future interests.

There are three types of future interest. These are as follows:

- A reversion to the grantor after a life estate or fee tail ends.
- A remainder to a third party after a life estate or fee tail ends.
- A possibility of reverter/ right of entry for condition broken given to the grantor in the case of a modified fee simple coming to an end.

Future interests have been encountered already in the context of freehold ownership (see Chapter 2). For example, in relation to conditional and determinable fee simples it was pointed out that if the condition or determining event occurs, the grantor can get back the fee simple estate himself either by exercising his right of entry for condition broken or by automatic reverter.

The grantor has an automatic reversion after a life estate or fee tail comes to an end. These interests are carved out of the fee simple so that when they come to an end the person who originally had the fee simple estate gets it back. Alternatively, the grantor can give his reversion to someone else. When an interest after a limited freehold estate is given to someone other than the grantor it is known as a remainder.

Most of the law we will be covering in this chapter relates to remainders. The law on future interests granted by an individual to himself is simple since there is no problem with their validity. The law

3/2158920

does not restrict reversions, rights of entry for condition broken or reverters. However, the law has acted so as to restrict remainders to third parties, particularly when they are contingent.

Contingent remainders are interests which may possibly arise in the future if certain conditions are fulfilled.

Vested remainders are interests where the holder of the interest is alive and ready to step into possession on determination of the prior estate.

Example: to Seamus for life, then to Debbie for life, then to Carol in fee simple if she becomes a headmistress

The gift to Seamus is not a future interest. It is a gift of a present right of ownership. It is granting Seamus an immediate estate over the land. The gift to Debbie is a future interest, but it is vested. Debbie is obviously a person who is alive at the time of the conveyance. If Seamus dies at any time, Debbie is ready to take possession of the land.

However, the gift to Carol is a contingent future interest. Even if the two prior estates end, this fact alone is not enough to give Carol a right to possession of the land. Her right only arises if, in addition, she has become a headmistress. Her interest is a contingent one because it will only arise on the satisfaction of some contingency other than the determination of all prior estates.

The distinction between vested and contingent interests will be discussed further below since it is important in applying the validity tests for remainders. It is very important to remember that a considerable amount of future interests are liable to be invalidated by the courts.

Over the years the law has developed a number of rules making remainders and gifts over invalid. Lawyers developed devices to avoid this, but the courts caught up with them and in turn imposed restrictions on these new devices.

Common law had very strict validity requirements for legal remainders. These requirements are known as the common law remainder rules. Lawyers initially employed the concept of the use to create remainders which were not subject to the common law remainder rules. When the Statute of Uses was passed these interests were converted into legal interests by the statute and became known as legal executory interests. Subsequently, the courts developed the separation of legal and equitable ownership again through the device of the

trust. The remainders created under a trust were known as future trusts. Neither future trusts nor legal executory interests were subject to the common law remainder rules. However, gradually they too were restricted by new rules, in particular the rule against perpetuities.

Having outlined the background to this topic it is necessary to pause and summarise the modern law on future interests before proceeding further:

- The main issue in relation to future interests is whether or not they are valid.
- The only future interests whose validity is in question are gifts to third parties, *i.e.* remainders.
- Different validity rules apply depending on whether the remainders are common law remainders, legal executory interests or future trusts.

Types of future interests and the validity rules which apply to them

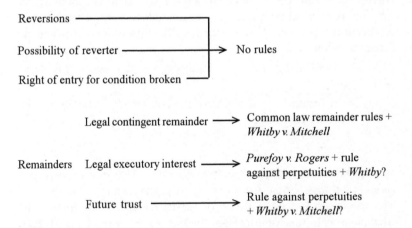

This diagram and the above summary should be kept in mind when studying this topic. The rest of this chapter expands upon the issues referred to in the chart.

II: Categories of Remainder: Important Distinctions

The distinction between vested and contingent remainders

It is necessary to know when a remainder is vested in order to apply the common law remainder rules and the rule against perpetuities. Most of the rules mentioned in the above chart do not invalidate vested interests. However, common law remainder rules (b) and (c) (see section III of this chapter) may apply to invalidate vested interests, as may the rule in *Whitby v. Mitchell* ((1890) 44 Ch. D. 85) as regards subsequent vested interests.

When someone has a right to the present enjoyment of land their interest is said to be vested in possession. This is a present and not a future interest. When someone has a present right to future enjoyment of land their interest is said to be vested in interest.

Example 1: to Robert for life, remainder to Brendan for life, remainder to Dan for life

Dan's interest is a future interest because it cannot give Dan a right to possession until Robert and Brendan's deaths, which have not yet occurred. But it can be said that if Robert and Brendan pass away at any time in his lifetime, Dan will have an immediate right of ownership. So his future interest is vested in interest. Two examples of contingent interests follow:

Example 2: to Mona for life, remainder to her eldest daughter in fee simple

Mona has no children at the time of the conveyance. The remainder to her daughter cannot be a vested interest because it fails to satisfy condition (a) above. It is a remainder in favour of someone who was not alive at the time it was created.

Example 3: to Greta for life, remainder to Marlene when she reaches the age of 21 (an inter vivos conveyance)

Marlene is aged 19 at the time of the conveyance. The interest to Marlene is a contingent interest at the time of the conveyance. It fails to satisfy condition (b) above. If Greta died the day after the conveyance, Marlene would not be able to claim an immediate right to possession because she would not yet have reached the age of 21. Marlene's interest is a contingent remainder at the time of the conveyance.

However, the courts prefer to construe interests as vested. Often, what might appear at first sight to be a contingent interest is construed as a vested interest subject to divesting on the occurrence of some contingency.

One example of this is the rule in *Edwards v. Hammond* ((1683) 3 Lev. 132) which applies only in the case of remainders created by will. The rule provides that if there is a remainder granted to someone who is alive at the time of the gift and that person's attaining a certain age is a condition precedent to the gift, then the gift is treated as vested, subject to being divested in the event of the subject failing to attain that age.

So, in relation to example 3, if the remainder to Marlene had been created by will, then the gift to Marlene would come within the exception in *Edwards v. Hammond* and be treated as vested subject to divesting if Marlene failed to reach 21 years.

Summary

A future interest can only be vested in interest if:

(a)   the person or persons who are entitled to it were alive at the time of its creation; and

(b)   the interest is so framed as to take effect in possession immediately once all previous estates have determined.

If a remainder fails to satisfy either of these conditions, then it is a contingent remainder.

The distinction between common law remainders, legal executory interests and future trusts

As can be seen from the above diagram (see p. 23), different validity rules apply depending whether the remainder or gift over is a common law remainder, a future trust or a legal executory interest. This section aims to clarify the distinction between these three categories.

A common law remainder is a remainder of the legal estate in the property. A disposition *"to A for life, remainder to C in fee simple"* would, for example, create such a remainder.

A legal executory interest, as demonstrated in the previous chapter, is a disposition whereby the legal estate in the property is granted to X to be held by him *"to the use of A for life, then to the use of C in fee simple"*. This disposition does not give C an ordinary legal remainder as it does not purport to grant a legal remainder in the property. The legal estate is intended to be held at all times by X, and C is only intended to have an equitable remainder. However, under the Statute of Uses, C's equitable estate or use is converted into a legal estate.

This remainder is distinguished from a straightforward legal remainder. It is known as a legal executory interest. C has a legal remainder, but only because his equitable interest was executed by the Statute of Uses. This is where the word "executory" comes in. So, if the conveyance to the remainderman does not have a use before it, it is a legal remainder. If it has one use only, it conveys a legal executory interest. If it contains a double use, as will be illustrated immediately below, it conveys an equitable interest/future trust.

As outlined in the previous chapter, the courts circumvented the Statute of Uses by the artificial mechanism of recognising a "use upon a use" as creating an equitable interest only. Therefore, if a conveyancer inserted a double use in a conveyance, the beneficiary of the second use merely received the equitable interest in the property. This mechanism is used by conveyancers today to create the modern trust. It represents the way in which trusts of future interests are currently created.

Thus, a disposition *"to A to the use of B to the use of C for life, remainder to the use of D in fee simple"* creates a future trust in favour of D, because there are two uses before the gift to D. For brevity's sake, this is often written in an attenuated form:

> *"Unto and to the use of A to the use of C for life, remainder to the use of D in fee simple".*

In the exam, the student may be required to decide whether a remainder is a common law remainder, a legal executory interest or a future trust. This can only be done by looking at the terms of the conveyance which created the remainder.

Summary
- If the conveyance contains no use, it is a common law remainder.
- If the conveyance contains "to the use of" before the remainder, it is a legal executory interest.
- If the conveyance creates a double use, by having the extra words "unto and to the use of X on trust for Y", then it creates a future trust.

III: LEGAL RESTRICTIONS ON REMAINDERS: THE VALIDITY RULES

The common law remainder rules

These only apply to common law remainders. They do not apply to reversions, possibility of reverter, or right to entry for breach of condition. The common law remainder rules derive from an era when tenure was prevalent and the concept of seisin very important. The common law felt that there must always be someone entitled to the legal estate in the land in order that the lord might have someone on whom to levy dues. Now, they have become to a large extent outdated.

In total, there are four common law remainder rules. They have two purposes: to prevent a gap in seisin (a period when no one has the right to a freehold estate in land) and to prevent an arbitrary shifting of ownership.

(a) A contingent remainder must be supported by a prior freehold estate

In other words, a gift "to Jessica when she obtains her Leaving Certificate" would fail under this rule. This is a contingent remainder if Jessica has not got the exam at the time of the conveyance. Because there is no prior gift before the gift to Jessica, there is no one who is entitled to the land during the period until Jessica obtains her Leaving Certificate and the gift vests. There is a gap in seisin and the common law will not allow this.

(b) Any remainder after a fee simple is void

(c) Any remainder is void if it cuts short a prior freehold estate

For example, take the case of the disposition "*to Robert for life, but if Mary becomes a doctor, to Mary in fee simple*". The gift to Mary is invalid under the above rule, because it cuts short Robert's life estate before the natural date of its determination, namely his death.

(d) A remainder is void if it does not vest during the continuance of the particular estate or at the moment of its duration

With this rule a "wait and see" principle is employed:

(i) If a gap in seisin is inevitable, then the interest is void from the outset at common law.

(ii)   If a gap in seisin is possible, but not certain, then it is per-
         missible to wait and see whether a gap will occur in practice
         or not.

However, after the Contingent Remainders Act 1877 it is possible
that if a common law remainder satisfies (a), (b) and (c) and does not
fall within (d)(i) it is automatically valid if it satisfies the rule against
perpetuities. It is not necessary to wait and see whether it actually vests
by the date of determination of the previous estate.

The rule in *Purefoy v. Rogers*

This has been abolished by the Contingent Remainders Act 1877. Prior
to 1877 it would have applied to legal executory interests, but not to
future trusts.

The rule was as follows: if a legal executory interest complied
with common law rules (a)–(d)(i), it had to satisfy (d)(ii). Illogically, if
the legal executory interest clearly breached the common law remainder rules (a) to (d)(i) it was a valid legal executory interest with no need
to worry about (d)(ii). Hence, drafters of legal executory interests
could avoid this rule by ensuring that the remainder breached the
common law from the outset.

As the Contingent Remainders Act 1877 abolished the rule in
Purefoy v. Rogers, it is no longer necessary to worry about it.

The rule in *Whitby v. Mitchell*

This is sometimes described as the old rule against perpetuities. It
applies to common law remainders. Its application to legal executory
interests and equitable future interests is undocumented by case law
and the leading Irish textbook writers appear to differ on this point.

The rule may be summarised as follows: if an interest in land is
given to an unborn person, any remainder in favour of his issue is void
together with all subsequent remainders, whether vested or contingent.

The rule in *Whitby v. Mitchell* was developed by the courts to
avoid the creation of unbarrable entails.

It does not apply to ordinary fee tail estates which are of course
barrable under the Fines and Recoveries (Ireland) Act 1834. There is
now no practical need for it, as unbarrable entails are effectively prohibited under the rule against perpetuities.

The rule is particularly harsh in so far as it invalidates not only the
gift to the issue of the unborn person, but also any gifts, vested or
not, which come after that gift.

In the case of gifts under wills, the courts sometimes operate a *cy-près* approach to get around the rule in *Whitby v. Mitchell*. For example, in the case of *"a gift to John for life, remainder to his son for life, remainder to his son's son for life"* the gift to John's grandson is void if John had no son at the date of the testator's death. However, when it is contained in a will, the courts sometimes treat this disposition as giving a fee tail to John.

The rule against perpetuities

This rule does not apply to common law remainders, but applies to legal executory interests and future trusts. It does not apply to a fee tail or to possibility of reverter/right of entry for breach of condition after a modified fee.

Again, it was developed to avoid transactions aimed at keeping land within the family; courts were not prepared to enforce dispositions which would render land inalienable for a long time into the future.

Like the rule in *Whitby v. Mitchell*, the rule against perpetuities only operates to strike down contingent remainders; it aims at preventing remoteness of vesting.

The rule against perpetuities is as follows: a remainder is void if there is any possibility at the outset that it will vest in interest after the expiration of the perpetuity period (life or lives in being plus 21 years).

It is very important when applying the rule against perpetuities to know when vesting in interest occurs (see above, page 25 for the distinction between vested and contingent interests).

If the gift is dependent on a contingency which, when viewed at the outset, is not certain to occur within the perpetuity period, then it is void. There is no wait and see potential under the rule against perpetuities. If there is even a possibility at the outset that the gift may vest outside the perpetuity period, then it is void. Thus, it does not matter when choosing the lives in being that some of them may live to a great age; you will not know this when assessing the validity of the gift.

Examples of dispositions which breach the rule against perpetuities

Contingent remainders in *inter vivos* conveyances often break the rule against perpetuities. There is a possibility of them vesting outside the perpetuity period.

Gifts to persons alive at the time of the disposition are valid even if they are premised on a contingency, because such persons are regarded as lives in being. The gifts must vest, if they vest at all, within the lifetime of these persons and so within the perpetuity period (life or lives in being plus 21 years).

Inter vivos dispositions

However, contingent remainders in favour of the grantor's children must be very carefully scrutinised if they occur in *inter vivos* dispositions. There is always the possibility that the grantor will have more children after the conveyance. Those children will not constitute lives in being and the gifts to them will vest outside the perpetuity period. If the gifts to the children are limited to take effect on or before their twenty-first birthday, they are acceptable. This is explained below.

Gifts to people who are not lives in being are dangerous unless such people are children of lives in being (or grandchildren of the testator if it is a will) and the gift is phrased to vest by the time they are 21. In all other cases where the gift is to someone who is not a life in being, a clause should be inserted saying that if the gift does not vest by a certain time (nominated life in being, often a member of royalty, plus 21 years) it should be invalid. For example, in *Re Villar* ([1929] 1 Ch. 243) it was stated that a contingent interest must vest within 20 years after the death of the last survivor of all lineal descendants of Queen Victoria alive at the date of the disposition in order to be valid.

These principles can be best illustrated by taking the example of an inter vivos conveyance by Elizabeth containing a remainder *"to my first daughter to attain the age of 25"*. At the time of the conveyance, Elizabeth has one daughter, aged 12 years. As this is an *inter vivos* conveyance, Elizabeth is still alive at the date of the conveyance and it is possible that she could bear another daughter. This child would not be a life in being at the time of the conveyance. If Elizabeth's eldest daughter died before reaching 18, the gift would vest in this second child more than 21 years after the end of the perpetuity period.

On the other hand, if the remainder was *"to my first daughter to attain the age of 21"* the gift would be acceptable. Elizabeth is a life in being at the time of the conveyance. Obviously, none of her children can attain 21 later than 21 years after her death, so the perpetuity period could not be exceeded. Similarly, *inter vivos* gifts to children of people who are alive at the time of the conveyance are fine so long as they are phrased to vest on or before the child's twenty-first birthday.

Returning to the first example given, what if Elizabeth could produce evidence from a doctor that at 60 years old she is past the age of childbearing? There is no possibility of her having another daughter and so the gift must vest, if it vests at all, within the perpetuity period. Either her existing daughter lives to be 18 years and the gift vests or, alternatively, her daughter dies before she reaches 18 years and the gift fails. Either way the gift must fail within six years, according to medical knowledge.

However, the rule against perpetuities does not make allowances for human biology. The rule against perpetuities does not provide any help for Elizabeth in the above situation. Instead, it employs the principle that all women, irrespective of their age or medical history, are theoretically capable of conceiving. This is known as "the fertile octogenarian fallacy". It finds a parallel in the "precocious toddler fallacy", also to be seen in the case law on the rule, which regards a two-year-old boy as capable of fathering a child. The absurdity of these two principles have led to much criticism of the rule against perpetuities. It is possible that they would not be followed by an Irish court.

Dispositions to children and grandchildren in wills are more likely to satisfy the rule against perpetuities than if such dispositions are contained in *inter vivos* dispositions. In the case of wills, dispositions to grandchildren of the testator (but not to grandchildren of anyone else) to take effect before they reach 21 will be valid. It is interesting to contrast this with the position regarding *inter vivos* dispositions.

Testamentary dispositions

Gifts to people alive at the time of the testator, *e.g.* parents, are permissible, because such people are necessarily lives in being, so the gift must vest, if it vests at all, in their lifetime.

Gifts to children of the testator are also allowed because such children necessarily constitute lives in being, being alive at the time of the testator's death (even if not yet born: a child *en ventre sa mère* qualifies as a life in being). Even if those gifts are conditional, *e.g.* *"to the first one of my children to become a solicitor"* they will be upheld because the contingency must necessarily happen in the lives of the children, who are lives in being.

Gifts to grandchildren in wills are permitted, so long as they are phrased so as to vest before the grandchild reaches the age of 21. This is because the parents of the grandchildren are lives in being, and the perpetuity period includes lives in being plus 21 years, and it is impossible for a child to reach 21 more than 21 years after their parent's death (except in one situation, with which the perpetuity rule has been adapted to deal).

For example, Madeleine makes a disposition in her will *"to my first grandchild to reach the age of 21"*. Madeleine has no grandchildren at the time of her death, but she has two children. If her children are alive at the time of her death, they qualify as lives in being. The perpetuity period is 21 years plus lives in being, so obviously Madeleine's grandchild, if she has one, is going to reach 21 within 21 years of the death of one of her children.

The perpetuity period may be extended to 21 years and nine months (nine months being the period of gestation of an infant) when necessary. Even if Madeleine's son dies after her, leaving his wife pregnant with their child, who is born six months later, the fact that the gift to that child vests 21 years and six months after the death of the life in being is not enough to void the gift, because the perpetuity period also includes any necessary period of gestation.

If a disposition is void under the perpetuities rule, what happens to subsequent gifts?

It was mentioned that the rule in *Whitby v. Mitchell* was particularly harsh because it operated to invalidate subsequent gifts even though they might be vested. The perpetuities rule may possibly eliminate subsequent gifts, but only if their vesting is dependent on the vesting of the vitiated gift:

- If the subsequent gift is vested from the outset this is valid.
- If the subsequent gift is contingent but independent and not vitiated by the perpetuities rule this is valid.
- If the subsequent gift is dependent on the validity of the previous gift, then it is obviously invalid. It will be contingent if it follows a gift of a determinable fee simple or a fee simple upon a condition.

The alternative contingencies exception

There is a special modification of the perpetuities rule whereby a gift may vest if one of two or more alternative contingencies is fulfilled, one of these contingencies being valid under the perpetuity rule and the other being invalid. It is permissible to wait and see which contingency is fulfilled first. If it is the contingency which breaches the perpetuity rule, then the gift fails, even though the vesting may have occurred within the perpetuity period. If it is the contingency which is valid under the perpetuity rule, then the gift is okay.

Other exceptions to the perpetuity rule

- The rule against perpetuities does not apply to possibilities of reverter/rights of entry for condition broken. These are rights which vest in the grantor of a determinable or conditional fee simple on its termination. However, if the grantor of a modified fee purports to grant a remainder over to another person if such estate ends, that remainder will be subject to the rule.
- The rule against perpetuities does not apply to remainders to third parties after a fee tail, provided that such remainders are certain to vest on the determination of the fee tail or before then.
- Dispositions in favour of charities.

Class gifts

A class gift occurs where there is a gift to a category of persons, anyone who satisfies the specified criteria being entitled to a share. The gift is not restricted to a single individual. If it is possible that an interest might vest in favour of any member of the class at a time beyond the perpetuity period, the gift in favour of the entire class will be void under the rule against perpetuities.

However, the courts have developed ways round this. The preferred solution is to apply the class-closing rules developed in the case of *Andrews v. Partington* ((1791) 3 Bro. C.C. 4012). This case lays down that where a class gift is void under the rule, it can be saved by presuming the grantor to have intended that the class should close as soon as an interest under the class vests in possession. No one who is born after an interest under the class vests in possession can constitute a member of the class.

Chapter 5

The Settled Land Acts 1882–90

This chapter on the Settled Land Acts follows logically from Chapter 2: Freehold Ownership and from Chapter 4: Future Interests.

The reason why the judiciary has restricted the creation of remainders and the legislature has intervened to allow the barring of the fee tail estate is because both these concepts restrict the alienation of land and conflict with the fundamental economic principle that land should be freely alienable (freely transferable or saleable).

The Settled Land Acts are also aimed at ensuring the free alienation of land. This legislation was primarily designed to make inalienable land (*e.g.* land subject to a succession of life estates followed by remainders, or land subject to a base fee) alienable. In addition, they also deal with another category of land in relation to which alienation was difficult, namely the property of minors.

There are three categories of land to which the Acts apply:

- Land held under a settlement.
- Land belonging to a minor.
- Land held under a trust for sale.

I: LAND HELD UNDER A SETTLEMENT

A settlement is any document creating successive legal or equitable interests in land.

Prior to the Settled Land Acts, there existed a concept known as the strict settlement which was aimed at keeping land in a particular family. This was usually achieved by a landowner giving land to his son for life and providing for a remainder in fee tail in favour of his son's eldest son. When the grandson came of age he could join with his father to bar the entail. However, until then the entail could not be barred.

Even when the entail was barred it was common practice to resettle the land again on similar lines. Successive strict settlements resulted in tying up land for generations. The land was not freely alienable and, often, could not be properly used. The main aim of the Settled Land Acts was to ensure the alienability of land which was subject to successive interests. Therefore, land held under a settlement catches within its terms the strict settlement. It also includes fee tails, base fees, estates *pur autre vie* and modified fee simples.

The Settled Land Acts allow transfer of such land free of any charges and/or future interests over it, such incumbrances being transferred to the purchase money received for the land.

The transfer of land subject to successive interests will be conducted by the tenant for life of that land.

The tenant for life was defined under section 2(5) of the 1882 Act as the person who is, at the time, beneficially entitled to possession for life under the settlement, *i.e.* the holder of a life estate.

The statutory definition of tenant for life also includes:

- tenant in fee tail;
- base fee;
- tenant *pur autre vie*;
- tenant in tail with possibility of issue extinct.

The powers of the tenant for life are as follows: he may sell the land or lease it. In certain limited circumstances, he may mortgage it. These powers cannot be excluded by the terms of the settlement.

However, the Settled Land Acts also put safeguards in place to prevent the powers of the tenant for life being abused. The interests of future beneficiaries under the settlement are protected by the doctrine of overreaching and by individuals known as the trustees of the settlement.

The doctrine of overreaching means that when settled land is sold or leased, future interests in the land are not extinguished, but rather transferred from the land to the money received for the transfer or lease.

The money received is known as capital money. It is paid by the purchaser not to the tenant for life but to individuals known as the trustees of the settlement. Their duty is to administer the purchase money according to the terms of the settlement.

Determining the trustees of the settlement involves asking a number of questions:

- Are there trustees under the original settlement with a power of sale/power to consent to a sale?
- If not, are there persons declared by the original settlement to be trustees of the settlement for the purposes of the Settled Land Acts?
- If not, are there persons with a power of sale of any other land comprised in the settlement apart from the land to be sold?
- If not, are there persons under the settlement with a future power of sale over the land?

If no one qualifies under the above test, then an application should be made to the court for the appointment of trustees of the settlement. Such trustees should be impartial.

If the purchaser does not pay the capital money to at least two trustees he will not take the property free of the future interests. If he does so, however, he will get an absolute title to the property.

Several other safeguards are worth noting:

- The tenant for life owes a fiduciary duty to the remaindermen to get the best price possible.
- The principal mansion house cannot be sold without the consent of the trustees of the settlement.
- The tenant for life has to give notice to the trustees of the settlement before he can exercise his powers.
- He has a duty to supply further information about the sale to the trustees on request.

II: LAND BELONGING TO A MINOR

There was difficulty with an minor transferring land during the period of his infancy because the law provided that any transfer of land by a minor was voidable by him within a reasonable time after his coming of age. Understandably, purchasers were reluctant to buy from an infant. Hence, his land was characterised as settled land under the Settled Land Act 1882. Although stretching the definition of settled land somewhat, the inclusion of infants' land accorded with the general policy behind the Act, namely that land should be freely alienable. The land held by the infant did not have to be subject to successive interests to come within the Act.

In the case of land belonging to a minor, the minor is the tenant for life. However, unlike the tenant for life of land subject to successive interests, he does not have the right to sell the land himself. Instead the sale is done for him by the trustees of the settlement.

III: LAND HELD UNDER A TRUST FOR SALE

The inclusion of this category within the definition of settled land has been criticised.

A trust for sale usually, but not necessarily, involved successive beneficial interests in land. However, the interests were beneficial interests under a trust and the trustees had the obligation to sell the land and hold the purchase money on the same trusts as had applied to the land.

The purpose of a trust for sale was directly opposite to the purpose of a strict settlement. Instead of trying to keep a particular piece of land in the family, it aimed to get rid of it. It was really strict settlements that the Settled Land Act 1882 was designed to circumvent. It is questionable whether land held under a trust for sale needed to be included within the terms of the Settled Land Act at all.

However, section 63 of the 1882 Act stated that land subject to a trust for sale should be deemed to be settled land, and that the person beneficially entitled under the trust for sale should be deemed to be tenant for life. The former trustees for sale were now reduced to the position of trustees of the settlement. The power of dealing with the land now lay in the hands of the tenant for life rather than the trustees for sale.

This caused an outcry and was amended by the Settled Land Act 1884 which allowed the trustees for sale to exercise the powers of the tenant for life without his consent. In addition, section 7 of the 1884 Act provided that the tenant for life under a trust for sale could not exercise the powers conferred on him by the 1882 Act without getting an order of the court. Once the court had issued an order allowing the tenant for life to exercise his powers, the trustees for sale could not exercise their powers while the order was in force.

The inclusion of trusts for sale in the Settled Land Act system creates serious problems, and ultimately serves to hinder the alienation of land.

Chapter 6

Co-ownership

A relationship of co-ownership arises where two or more persons have a simultaneous entitlement to a particular piece of land.

I: THE FORMS OF CO-OWNERSHIP

For the purposes of most university land law courses there are two forms of co-ownership, the joint tenancy and the tenancy in common.

Joint tenancy

Under a joint tenancy, each co-owner forms part of a single unit holding the land. When one joint tenant dies, a system known as survivorship applies, whereby that joint tenant's share passes to the remaining joint tenants rather than to the beneficiaries under his will or on intestacy. When all the joint tenants except one have died, the last remaining joint tenant gets the lot.

In order for co-owners to hold as joint tenants, the principles of the "unit" mechanism must be followed. There must be unity of time, place, interest and possession as between the joint tenants. These requirements are known as the four unities and need to be known in some detail.

Unity of Possession

Each joint tenant has the right to any part of the co-owned land. One joint tenant does not have the right to fence off a particular part and exclude the other joint tenants from it.

Unity of Interest

Each joint tenant must have the same estate in the land. There cannot be a joint tenancy if one co-owner has a life estate and the other has a fee simple. However, there can be a tenancy in common in such circumstances.

Unity of Title

All of the co-owners' interests must have been created by the same document or transaction.

Unity of Time

All of the co-owners' interests must have vested in interest at the same time. See Chapter 4: Future Interests for an explanation of the concept of vesting in interest.

If the four unities are not present, there cannot be a joint tenancy, only a tenancy in common.

A joint tenancy can be terminated by one of the recognised methods for terminating co-ownership, or it can be converted into a tenancy in common by severance.

Severance of a joint tenancy at common law occurs when one or more of the four unities are lost. There are also a number of additional situations in which equity regards a joint tenancy as having been severed but the common law does not. When there is severance of a joint tenancy in equity but not at common law the legal estate is held on a joint tenancy but the equitable estate is held on a tenancy in common

Situations where the legal estate is held according to one form of co-ownership and the equitable estate is held on another form of co-ownership are quite common. Equity favours a tenancy in common; the common law favours a joint tenancy.

Tenancy in common

A tenancy in common is a form of co-ownership whereby each tenant in common is regarded as holding a separate share in the co-owned land.

However, obviously the land has not been divided up to reflect these separate shares; if it had there would be no co-ownership at all. The essence of a tenancy in common is that each tenant in common has a distinct, independent but undivided share. Shares of tenants in common need not be equal in value. However, if a joint tenancy is severed and turned into a tenancy in common, each former joint tenant takes an equal share as tenant in common.

The four unities need not be present for a tenancy in common. Only one of them need be present, namely unity of possession. This unity is necessary for any form of co-ownership to exist.

Having distinguished between a joint tenancy and a tenancy in common, we now need to investigate the following issue which tends to feature regularly in exam problems: If two people are co-owners of property, how is it decided whether they hold under a joint tenancy or a tenancy in common?

The first step towards resolving this issue is to look at the way in which the co-ownership came into being in the first place. It is necessary to know the respective requirements for creating a joint tenancy/tenancy in common.

II: CREATION OF A JOINT TENANCY/TENANCY IN COMMON

Joint tenancy

For a joint tenancy to be created at common law:

(a)   The four unities must be present.

(b)   There must be no words of severance in the conveyance. Words of severance are words indicating each co-owner is to take a distinct share in the property. As such they are inconsistent with the existence of a joint tenancy. Joint tenants' shares are only assessed when the joint tenancy is turned into a tenancy in common by severance. Examples of words of severance are "equally", "in equal shares", etc.

(c)   It must not fall into any of the situations recognised by equity as grounding a tenancy in common, otherwise there will be a tenancy in common of the equitable estate. These situations are as follows:

(i)   Where co-owners contribute to the purchase price in unequal shares.

(ii)   Where property is acquired by a partnership.

(iii) Where property is conveyed to a number of people in return for a loan.

(iv)   In *Malayan Credit v. Jack Chia-MPH Ltd.* ([1986] A.C. 549) it was emphasised that these categories are not closed and that new situations may arise in the future where equity will be prepared to recognise a tenancy in common.

Tenancy in common

A tenancy in common of the legal estate is created when one of the four unities is absent or there are words of severance in the conveyance. If the legal estate is held on tenancy in common then the equitable estate will always be held on tenancy in common. However, even if the legal estate is held on a joint tenancy there will still be a tenancy in common of the equitable estate if any of the four situations in (c) above are satisfied.

These are the tests which ought to be applied in deciding whether a particular form of co-ownership is created at the outset. However, that form of co-ownership may not necessarily have remained present, since a joint tenancy can be converted into a tenancy in common in a number of situations.

III: SEVERANCE OF A JOINT TENANCY

Even assuming that the form of co-ownership originally created was a joint tenancy, that does not settle the issue in problem questions; it may be necessary to further decide whether that joint tenancy has been *severed* at any time since its creation.

Common law treats a joint tenancy as being converted into a tenancy in common where one of the four unities is lost. If this can be proven then a joint tenancy will be converted into a tenancy in common both at law and in equity. For example, if one of the joint tenants acquires a greater estate in the land then there will be no unity of interest. Alternatively, if one of the joint tenants conveys his interest to a third party who was not a co-owner there will be no unity of title. This applies even if the conveyance has been by operation of law. In the case of *Containercare (Ireland) Ltd. v. Wycherley* ([1982] I.R. 143) the court granted a judgment mortgage over co-owned property. It was held that this had the effect of severing the joint tenancy.

However, even if the four unities remain, equity treats a joint tenancy as being severed in three additional situations. If these situations are present, the legal estate will remain held on a joint tenancy but the equitable estate will be held in tenancy in common.

The relevant situations were laid down in *Williams v. Hensman* ((1861) 1 J. & H. 546) and affirmed by an Irish judge in *Byrne v. Byrne* (unreported, High Court, January 18, 1980). They are as follows:

- Where a joint tenant enters into a contract to transfer his land to someone else.
- Where there is a mutual agreement between the joint tenants to sever.

- Where joint tenants behave in a manner which indicates that they now regard themselves as holding under a tenancy in common.

IV: DETERMINATION OF CO-OWNERSHIP

There are a number of ways in which a situation of co-ownership may come to an end.

Union in a sole tenant

This occurs either through survivorship or through one tenant buying out the other.

Partition

Partition is the physical division of the property. It must be done by deed. The court may have general equitable jurisdiction to order a partition if all the co-owners will not consent to it.

Sale in lieu of partition

Section 4 of the Partition Act 1868 provides that if requested by one of the co-owners the court shall order a sale of the co-owned property, unless it sees good reason to the contrary.

Chapter 7

Leasehold Ownership

Leasehold ownership is the right to exclusive possession of land, normally for a limited period, under an agreement with its owner to hold as landlord and tenant.

The freehold owner of land, *i.e.* the person owning the fee simple in the land, grants possession of the land to someone else who is known as the tenant. The tenant has the right to exclusive possession of the land for the duration of the lease. The tenant is known as the leasehold owner of the land. The landlord is the freehold owner.

In most leases, the landlord has what is known as a reversion. When the period of the lease or tenancy comes to an end, he has a right to get the property back. Hence, the creation of a lease is not the same as a transfer of freehold ownership. First, because a leasehold relationship gives rise to special rights on the part of the landlord, for example the right to forfeiture and the right to rent. Secondly, because the landlord usually gets the property back at the end of the period of the lease.

I: TYPES OF LANDLORD/TENANT RELATIONSHIPS

- A fixed term lease is a lease for a definite period, *e.g.* 21 years. Under Deasy's Act 1860, a lease may last forever.
- A periodic tenancy is a tenancy for a particular period, *e.g.* a week, a month or a year. It will be automatically renewed at the end of the period unless either party demonstrates their intention to terminate it by serving a notice to quit.
- A tenancy at will arises when a fixed term lease comes to an end and the tenant overholds with the consent of the landlord but without paying regular rent.
- A tenancy at sufferance arises when a lease or tenancy comes to an end and the tenant stays on in the premises without the assent or dissent of the landlord.

II: Creation of a Landlord/Tenant Relationship

Following Deasy's Act, a leasehold relationship is deemed to be created wherever there is a valid agreement between parties to create a landlord/tenant relationship, such agreement involving periodic payments known as rent.

In deciding whether a landlord/tenant relationship has been created, the first question which has to be asked is whether the parties intended to create the relationship of landlord and tenant between themselves. Secondly, if such an agreement exists, it has to be asked whether it is valid under contract law. Thirdly, it is necessary to consider whether the statutory writing formalities have been fulfilled.

Agreement to create a landlord/tenant relationship

The concept of the landlord/tenant relationship is based on the notion of an agreement between two parties, the landlord and the tenant. They must first of all agree to create a landlord/tenant relationship and not any other kind of relationship, for example a licence. A licence would only confer a personal right to possession and not a proprietary right. It would not carry with it any of the statutory rights and obligations which attach to the landlord/tenant relationship. Sometimes it may be difficult to distinguish an agreement for a licence from an agreement for a lease or tenancy.

The leading Irish case is *Irish Shell v. Costello* ([1981] I.L.R.M. 66). In this case, an agreement was described as a licence but contained certain clauses more appropriate to a lease. For example, there was a clause prohibiting the tenant from assigning his interest. If the document truly was a licence, there would be no need to include such a clause because a licence is not a proprietary right and cannot be assigned to third parties. In addition, it was pointed out that previous agreements between the parties had stated that there was no exclusive possession but that the agreement in question did not contain such a clause. Exclusive possession is necessary for a lease but is not on its own sufficient, as some licences involve exclusive possession. However, in the context of the agreement as a whole, the assignment clause and the exclusive possession indicated that the agreement was a lease.

Therefore, Irish courts are prepared to look behind the name tags assigned to the particular agreement. However, they hold exclusive possession to be an essential feature of a lease and if it is not present on the face of the agreement the agreement cannot be a lease and must be a licence.

The United Kingdom courts have gone one step further. In *Antoniades v. Villiers* ([1990] 1 A.C. 417) there was a clause in the agreement which negated exclusive possession; the agreement related to the right to use a flat and was entered into between a young couple and the owner of the building. The clause in the agreement stated that the landlord had the right to put someone else into the flat. However, it was clear that in practice this clause would never be exercised. There was only one bed in the flat, and the landlord had clearly inserted the clause to prevent the agreement being held to be a lease. In the circumstances the court treated the clause negating exclusive possession as a sham and held the agreement to be a lease.

This has not been the case in Ireland. If there is a clause in the agreement which expressly says that there is no exclusive possession the Irish courts are not prepared to look behind it and see whether it is intended to operate in practice. For example in *Governors of National Maternity Hospital, Dublin v. McGouran* ([1994] 1 I.L.R.M. 521) there was an agreement entered into by the hospital granting an individual the right to use part of the hospital as a coffee shop. The issue was whether the agreement was a lease or a licence. There was a clause in the agreement stating that the coffee shop "licensee" had no exclusive possession and that the hospital had the right to come on to the premises at any time they liked. On this basis the High Court held the agreement to be a licence. However, Morris J. does not appear to have engaged in any attempt to look behind the agreement and see whether the clause was intended to operate in practice. If it was intended to operate in practice, why did the hospital not have their own key to the shop? On the facts, the coffee shop "licensee" was the sole keyholder.

A similar approach was taken in *Kenny Homes & Co. Ltd. v. Leonard* (unreported, High Court, December 11, 1997). The High Court attitude on this point is questionable to some extent. *Irish Shell v. Costello* indicates that you cannot get a licence just by putting the word "licence" at the top of your agreement. However, the present approach of the Irish courts seems to be that although a landowner cannot secure a licence by inserting the one word "licence" in an occupation agreement, he may achieve this aim by inserting the five words "there is no exclusive possession".

The agreement must be valid under contract law

An agreement to create a landlord/tenant relationship must be valid under contract law. There must be a valid offer and acceptance, and the agreement must not have been secured subject to duress, undue influence or mistake. Furthermore, it must not be too vague. If it is a lease for a term certain, the term must be certain. *Lace v. Chantler* ([1944] 1 All E.R. 305) was a United Kingdom case where there was a lease for the duration of the war. This was held to be void for uncertainty.

The necessary writing requirements must be fulfilled

Finally, there are certain writing requirements which must be fulfilled in order to create a landlord/tenant relationship. Unless the lease is for year to year or any lesser period, it has to be in writing under Deasy's Act. Otherwise it cannot be a valid lease at common law.

The Deasy's Act writing requirement does not apply to yearly, weekly or monthly tenancies. It is an unresolved issue whether it applies to a lease for one year certain. Case law is divided on the issue of whether a tenancy for one year certain is for a lesser period than a yearly tenancy. In *Wright v. Tracey* ((1874) 8 I.R.C.L. 478) it was held that a tenancy for one year certain was not less than a tenancy from year to year and as such needed to be in writing. However, there has been criticism of this case in the decisions of *Jameson v. Squire* ([1948] I.R. 153) and *Bernays v. Prosser* ([1963] 2 All E.R. 321).

What happens if an agreement fails to satisfy the necessary writing requirements under Deasy's Act? Then you may try to enforce it in equity as an agreement to create a lease. This is known as the principle in *Walsh v. Lonsdale* ((1882) 21 Ch.D.9). Equity treats an agreement to create a lease as being as good as a lease. But in order to do this, it is necessary to show either the fulfilment of writing requirements sufficient to satisfy the Statute of Frauds or an act of part performance.

It is worth noting, however, that writing requirements under the Statute of Frauds are slightly different from writing requirements under Deasy's Act and this may be of some benefit. For example, under the Statute of Frauds the note in writing need not be made at the same time as the oral agreement is concluded. Under Deasy's Act, on the other hand, the note in writing must be contemporaneous with the oral agreement. Secondly, under the Statute of Frauds, the note in writing only has to be signed by the party to be charged on it. In contrast, under Deasy's Act the note in writing has to be signed by the landlord. Thirdly, under the Statute of Frauds an agent who signs does not have to have written authorisation.

Part performance occurs in the following situations: when the tenant goes into possession and pays rent or expends money on improvements. It may be difficult to show part performance when a previous tenant continues in possession under a new lease which is not in writing. Some variation in the payment of rent may suffice. In *McCausland v. Murphy* ((1881) 9 L.R. Ir. 9) the tenant had taken possession and carried out alterations. This was held to be a sufficient act of part performance.

Nonetheless, it has to be said that an equitable lease is not as good as a legal lease in certain respects. For example, the enforcement of an equitable lease depends on the availability of the equitable remedy of specific performance, which is a discretionary remedy. Secondly, easements will not pass with the lease either under *Wheeldon v. Burrows* ((1879) 12 Ch. D. 31) or under the Conveyancing Act 1881 because an equitable lease is not a conveyance for the purposes of those rules. (See below, Chapter 8: Easements for more about these rules.) Thirdly, the holder of an equitable lease may be bound by prior equitable interests and, finally, his leasehold interest may be lost if there is a sale of the freehold to a bona fide purchaser for value without notice.

What happens if there is neither a legal nor an equitable lease because the writing formalities are not fulfilled and there is no part performance? In this situation the original agreement cannot take effect.

If the tenant goes into possession and pays rent there may be a periodic tenancy, depending on the method used for paying the rent. If the tenant goes into possession with the consent of the landlord and does not pay rent he is a tenant at will. A tenant at will becomes an adverse possessor after one year.

III: CHARACTERISTICS OF LEASES

There are some basic characteristics of leases. For example, the tenant has the obligation to pay rent and the right to exclusive possession. The landlord has the obligation to stay out of the property during the duration of the lease. These obligations may be modified by express or implied clauses in the agreement. For example, in written leases the tenant has an implied duty to repair at common law. However, statute has also intervened to modify express duties contained in the written agreement. This is particularly the case in respect of the application of the Landlord and Tenant Amendment Act 1980 to leases involving tenements.

The landlord's duties under the lease

- The landlord has a duty to stay away for the duration of the lease except for situations expressly or impliedly stipulated in the lease or by statute. For example, he may have a right to come in to perform certain duties imposed on him by the lease.
- The landlord may have a very limited duty to repair at common law or statute. In relation to furnished lettings he has a duty to have the property in good repair at the date of commencement of the lease. As regards unfurnished lettings, if they are dwellings within the terms of the Housing (Private Rented Dwellings) Regulations 1993, the landlord has the duty to keep the dwelling in good structural repair and to look after common areas such as sinks, baths and showers.

If the landlord is a housing authority it has a duty to keep the premises fit for habitation; this was recognised in the case of *Siney v. Dublin Corporation* ([1980] I.R. 400) in which it was held that, in all contracts completed under the Housing Act 1966 between housing authorities and their lessees, there is an implied term that the premises will be fit for human habitation.

The landlord's duty to repair may be extended by express clauses in the lease.

- The landlord may have other duties expressly imposed on him by the terms of the lease, particularly in relation to insurance.

If the landlord breaches any of these duties he can be sued for damages/injunction/specific performance by the tenant.

The tenant's duties under the lease

- The tenant has a duty to pay the rent. As explained above, this is a necessary component of any landlord/tenant relationship.
- In addition, under a written lease the tenant has an implied statutory duty to repair and all tenants have a statutory duty to avoid waste. More extensive duties of repair may expressly be provided for in the lease.

Every tenant is liable at common law for permissive or voluntary waste unless the lease specifically excludes such liability. Waste is defined as damage done to property or the landlord's reversion by someone having a limited interest in the property.

The statutory duty to repair is implied by section 42 of Deasy's Act into all written agreements of tenancy. It is a covenant to keep premises in good and substantial repair and condition. It may be rebutted by a contrary statement in the lease.

There are a number of cases on the express/implied duties of repair imposed on the tenant.

In *Groome v. Fodhla Printing Co. Ltd.* ([1943] I.R. 380) there was a problem with the roof of the premises and the only way to fix it was to put in new supports. It was held that the tenant was obliged to do this. Black J. said that some repairs may necessarily involve inevitable improvements. A tenant cannot be excused from doing a repair simply because it enhances the letting value of the property. He may be obliged to give back a better house than he received. He may have to make structural repairs even though the structural defects were present at the time of the lease, if these defects are causing additional damage.

However, some cases exhibit a more relaxed approach. In *Whelan v. Madigan* ([1978] I.L.R.M. 136) there was a serious structural defect, namely, lack of adequate damp proofing. This led to damp creeping up the walls of the flat. It was held that the tenant was not liable to repair. His liability did not extend to defects caused by a structural defect present at the time of entering into the lease. This case appears to differ from *Groome v. Fodhla Printing Co. Ltd.* However, in *Whelan* there was an express provision in the lease indicating that the tenant's duty to repair was confined to keeping the interior of the flat in good condition. Interpreting the scope of the duty to repair involves looking at the terms of the repair covenant in the context of the lease as a whole and this was in fact recognised by Black J. in *Groome*.

- Other duties on the tenant have to be imposed expressly. Express covenants restricting the use to which the property may be put, and/or restricting assignment or subletting are common in leases.

The tenant is obliged to observe all his duties and if he does not he may be thrown out if the forfeiture conditions are satisfied or at the very least sued for forfeiture or an injunction.

However, some of the duties imposed on tenants were considered to be very harsh by the legislature and for this reason the Landlord and Tenant (Amendment) Act 1980 was enacted which modified the tenant's duties somewhat in the case of leases of tenements.

A tenement is a property which consists wholly or partly of buildings, with any part of the property not covered by buildings being merely subsidiary and ancillary to the buildings. Consequently, the term applies mainly to urban land, *e.g.* a house with a garden would be included in the definition because the garden could be said to be ancillary to the house.

It is very important to remember that these statutory modifications only apply to tenements and not to agricultural land.

- Section 65 of the Landlord and Tenant (Amendment) Act 1980 is a very important provision which significantly modifies the tenant's liability to pay damages for breach of a repair covenant. It only applies to tenements. It does not limit the landlord's right to forfeiture for breach of a repairing covenant.

Section 65 is divided into subsections (2) and (3). Subsection (2) restricts the amount of damages recoverable. It provides that the damages recoverable by the landlord from the tenant cannot exceed the amount by which the value of the lessor's reversion has been diminished.

Subsection (3) limits the circumstances in which damages may be recoverable. It provides that damages are not recoverable from the tenant for breach of a repairing covenant in three situations:

(a)   Where repair is physically impossible.
(b)   Where repair would involve disproportionate expenditure in relation to the value of the tenement.
(c)   Where the tenement could not be profitably used on repair.

However, there is also an important qualification to subsection (3); it does not apply, even in the three situations detailed above, if the want of repair is due wholly or substantially to wilful damage or wilful waste committed by the lessee. Note that this qualification only applies to subsection (3) and not subsection (2).

- Section 66 of the Act relates to covenants restricting or prohibiting assignment or sub-letting. It provides that if a landlord

uses these covenants to refuse consent to an assignment or sub-
letting he must be shown to be acting reasonably. Doubts about
the solvency of the proposed assignee constitute a reasonable
ground for refusing consent. Another acceptable ground may
be that of good estate management.

- Section 67 of the Act relates to covenants restricting the use to
  which the land may be put by the tenant. As with sections 65
  and 66, it only applies to tenements. As with section 66, it provides that a landlord may not invoke such covenants unreasonably. There are a number of cases defining unreasonableness in
  the context of section 67.

In *Rice v. Dublin Corporation* ([1947] I.R. 425) there was a covenant in
the lease of a tenement prohibiting the premises from being used as a
pub or a brothel. It was held on the facts that the landlord was acting
unreasonably in refusing his consent to the use of the premises as a
pub. There was no evidence that Dublin Corporation had a policy as
to the correct number of licenced premises in that neighbourhood. In
the absence of a clear policy, refusal of consent was unreasonable.
Limiting the number of pubs in an area might be reasonable, but
excluding them altogether was not.

However, in contrast with *Rice* there are a number of cases relating to covenants restricting user of units in shopping centres. In all
these cases a landlord's refusal of consent to a change in user was held
reasonable on the ground of estate management.

In *Greene Property v. Shalaine Modes* ([1978] 1 I.L.R.M. 222) it was a
term of a lease of a unit in a shopping centre that the premises would
be used as a hardware store. User was changed to a women's bou-
tique without objection from the landlord, and then to a toy shop.
The owner of another toy shop within the centre objected, which
prompted the landlord to refuse his consent to the change of use. It
was held that the landlord was reasonable in refusing his consent. The
lessor in a shopping centre has a financial interest in maintaining a
good mix of shops. The more attractive the shopping centre, the
higher the rents he could charge.

This approach was replicated in *Wanze Properties (Ireland) Ltd. v.
Mastertron Ltd.* ([1992] I.L.R.M. 746). Here the lessor objected to the
opening of a Chinese takeaway in the premises which were the subject of the lease. He argued that the Chinese takeaway would have
"dead frontage" which was a disadvantage in a shopping centre. He

also pointed out that such a business operated mainly in the evening so that it was closed when most of the shops in the centre were open, and open when they were closed. His refusal of consent was held reasonable.

IV: STATUTORY RIGHTS OF THE TENANT

The legislature has done more than modify the tenant's duties. It has also conferred on the tenant certain rights which have the result of significantly diminishing the landlord's freehold interest in certain circumstances. These statutory rights are three-fold in nature:

- The right to a new tenancy.
- The right to a reversionary lease/fee simple.
- Rights under rent control legislation.

The right to a new tenancy

This is granted by Part II of the Landlord and Tenant (Amendment) Act 1980 and only applies in respect of tenements. In addition to the land being a tenement the person claiming the right must show the existence of one of three equities:

Business equity
This arises if there has been continuous occupation as a business for five years (three years if the lease was entered into before August 10, 1994). The term "business" includes social, cultural, sporting activities, or the practice of a profession. The activity does not have to be carried on for reward to qualify as a business.

Long user equity
This arises after 20 years continuous occupation. However, if the tenant has purchased his leasehold interest during this time he cannot rely on this equity.

Improvement equity
This occurs if half or more of the letting value of the tenement is due to an improvement made by the tenant.

Exclusions from the right to a new tenancy

Certain types of leases are excluded from entitlement to this right. Examples are non-business leases of local authority property, State property and property in the Custom House Docks Area.

Restrictions on the right to a new tenancy

In addition, there are certain grounds on which the right to a new tenancy may legitimately be refused even if the above conditions are fulfilled. Some examples follow:

- If the tenancy has been terminated for non-payment of rent or breach of covenant.
- If the landlord wants the property for rebuilding, a scheme of development or good estate management.
- If the landlord is a planning authority and the building is in an obsolete area scheduled for renewal under the Urban Development Plan.

The extent of the right

If the tenant satisfies the criteria for the grant of a new tenancy, the court fixes the terms of the new tenancy. It should be 35 years or less in duration, and if the tenancy arises through a business equity it should be for 20 years or less. The rent fixed is the gross rent, namely that rent which a willing lessee would give and a willing lessor would take on the basis of vacant possession.

Obtaining a fee simple/reversionary lease

The right to buy out the fee simple allows the tenant to purchase the landlord's freehold interest. A reversionary lease is a lease for a very long time (99 years), at a low rent, which is automatically renewable.

A fee simple is obtained under the Landlord and Tenant (Ground Rents) Acts 1967–87 whereas a reversionary lease is obtained under the Landlord and Tenant (Amendment) Act 1980; but the criteria for obtaining the two rights are substantially the same. There are some differences, but it is easier to deal with both rights together, pointing out the differences in the process.

It is best to start by distinguishing between oral and written tenancies. As regards oral tenancies, it is only possible to obtain the fee simple under the Ground Rents Act, since Part III of the 1980 Act does not apply to oral tenancies.

It is possible to obtain the fee simple of an oral lease under the Ground Rents Acts if the following four conditions are satisfied:

(a) where the lessee has a yearly lease;
(b) where there are permanent buildings on the land, the land is

subsidiary and ancillary to the buildings and the buildings were not erected in breach of covenant;

(c) where either:
  (i) the buildings were erected by the lessee or his predecessor in title under the lease; or
  (ii) the lessee has had possession for 25 years or more at a low rent and the lessor is not in a position to prove that he erected the buildings;

(d) none of the restrictions on obtaining a fee simple apply. These restrictions are not dissimilar to the restrictions on obtaining the right to a new tenancy referred to above.

As regards written tenancies, it is possible to get a fee simple/reversionary lease if:

(a) there are permanent buildings on the land, the land is be subsidiary and ancillary to the buildings, the buildings are not an improvement and they have not been erected in breach of a covenant in the lease;

(b) one of the following conditions applies:
  (i) the buildings were erected by the lessee or his predecessor in title. (If the lease was for 50 plus years at a low rent there is a presumption that the buildings were erected by the present lessee or his predecessors in title);
  (ii) the initial lease was a lease to someone nominated by the builder of the buildings;
  (iii) the lease was granted on the expiry or surrender of an earlier lease which qualified for a fee simple or reversionary lease under the Acts;
  (iv) a reversionary lease has already been granted;
  (v) the lease was for 50 plus years and was granted partly in consideration of a lump sum or substantial expenditure by the lessee on matters other than decoration;

(c) none of the restrictions on reversionary leases/fee simples are applicable. These restrictions are similar to the restrictions on the grant of a new tenancy.

Rights attaching to controlled dwellings

A controlled dwelling is a house or a flat the rateable valuation of which was below a certain level in 1982. Certain dwellings are excluded, for example self-contained flats made after 1960 and modern dwellings built after May 7, 1941. There is provision for premises to become decontrolled if the tenant assigns or sublets or the landlord recovers possession.

An individual who was a tenant of a controlled dwelling in 1982 has the right to stay there all his life. The spouse of such a person, if residing in the dwelling at the time of his death, has the right to remain there for the rest of her life. A member of the family residing in the dwelling at the time of either the tenant's death or the death of the tenant's spouse is entitled to remain in the property until 2002. The landlord may exceptionally recover possession if the tenancy becomes decontrolled or if he requires the property for a specific purpose.

V: Methods of Terminating a Lease

Expiry

A fixed term lease comes to an end when the term of the lease runs out. Additionally, there are rules in the Statute of Limitation 1957 providing that a tenancy at will automatically expires after one year and that a tenancy from year to year which is not in writing will end at the end of the first year.

Surrender

Surrender occurs when the tenant under a fixed term lease conveys his leasehold interest back to the landlord before the expiry of the lease. For a surrender to be valid, it ought to satisfy section 7 of Deasy's Act by being a note in writing signed by the tenant. Sometimes a surrender will be implied from the acts of the parties in cases where section 7 is not satisfied. It is important to remember that a lessee does not have an automatic right to surrender. He must be given that right by statute, by the lease, or by the agreement of the landlord.

Merger

Merger occurs when the leasehold and freehold interest become vested in either the tenant or a third party. Before merger can occur, there must be an additional intention on the part of the new owner to merge the two estates. This is demonstrated by the case of *Craig v. Greer* ([1899] 1 I.R. 258). Here a sub-lease provided that the sub-lessees were bound by covenants contained in the head lease. The sub-lessor subsequently acquired the estate of the head lessor. It was argued that this brought about a merger which destroyed his rights under the sub-lease and the covenants, and so they no longer bound the sub-lessees. The court held that it had not been the intention of the sub-lessor to bring about a merger, as such a merger would have destroyed his rights under the sub-lease.

Frustration

The contractual doctrine of frustration applies to leases. In the context of a lease, destruction of a house is probably not enough to terminate a lease. In order for the contract to be frustrated, the actual land would have to be destroyed, *e.g.* by subsidence into the sea.

There is a statutory frustration clause contained in section 40 of Deasy's Act. Where a dwelling house is destroyed by fire or inevitable accident the tenant may surrender the lease. However, this clause is of little practical importance because it only applies if the lease does not contain an express covenant to repair. Most leases contain such a covenant.

Notice to quit

This is the most common way of terminating periodic tenancies. Periodic tenancies continue indefinitely and will normally only end if either the landlord or the tenant serves a notice to quit.

A document will satisfy the definition of a notice to quit if it amounts to a clear and unambiguous communication of an intention to end the tenancy at the determination of a specified period. Once the period has come to an end, the tenancy determines.

It is preferable that the notice to quit should be in writing, but this is not compulsory. Furthermore, extra requirements may have to be satisfied if the agreement of tenancy provides that any notice to quit should be in a specified form. Statute further requires that a notice to quit in relation to agricultural land should be in writing and signed, and that a notice to quit residential accommodation must be in writing and delivered at least four weeks in advance of the date on which the notice period runs out.

The notice period which is necessary

One week's notice is necessary to end a weekly tenancy. If the weekly tenancy is residential, then, under the Housing Act 1992, four weeks' notice must be given. At least one month's notice must be given to end a monthly tenancy. To end a yearly tenancy a half-year's (183 days') notice is needed.

These periods are often extended in practice, however, because of rules relating to expiry of the notice. A notice to quit must expire at the end of a period of tenancy in order to be valid. Take the example of a weekly tenancy which started on a Monday. In a situation where the landlord decides on a Wednesday to get rid of his tenant, it is not permissible for him merely to give the tenant notice that day and expect him to have left the premises by the following Wednesday. The notice to quit must give at least a week's notice and be framed so as to expire on the last day of the period of tenancy. Thus, even if he serves on a Wednesday time does not begin to run until the following Monday and the tenant does not have to leave until Monday week (or Monday four weeks if he has a residential tenancy).

For this reason it is important to know the exact date on which the tenancy commenced. If this is not known, it is best to look at the gale day, which is the day on which the rent is paid. In *Lynch v. Dolan* ([1973] I.R. 319) there was a weekly tenancy. The date of commencement of the tenancy was not known, but the rent was paid on a Friday. So notice to quit served on a Friday to quit on the next Friday was acceptable. If the commencement of a yearly tenancy is not known, there is a presumption that it commences on the last gale day of any calendar year.

Forfeiture

If there is a breach of a covenant in the lease the landlord can always bring an action for damages. However, this may not always be sufficient to prevent future breaches. Forfeiture allows the landlord to terminate the lease early for breach of covenant if four conditions are fulfilled. These conditions are as follows:

(a) The covenant must be one a breach of which entitles the landlord to forfeit

In other words, the covenant must either be expressed to be a condition of the lease or there must be an express forfeiture clause attached to it saying that there is the right to forfeiture if it is breached. Something will normally be regarded as a condition if it is introduced by wording such as "on condition that" or "provided that". Most leases have a clause providing for forfeiture if a tenant fails to perform any of his covenants.

(b) The covenant must be breached

(c) A forfeiture notice must be served on the tenant under section 14(1) of the Conveyancing Act 1881

This notice must specify the breach, and whether the tenant is required to remedy the breach or pay compensation. The landlord must give the tenant a reasonable time to comply with the forfeiture notice.

A forfeiture notice is not necessary where the covenant breached is one relating to the non-payment of rent. This is set out under section 14(8) of the Conveyancing Act 1881. In such cases the only obligation on the landlord is to comply with the common law and make a demand for the rent. The need for a demand for the rent may be excluded by the terms of the lease.

(d) There must be some act of forfeiture on the part of the landlord

This would be effected either by:

(i)   the initiation of legal proceedings through an action for ejectment on the title; or

(ii)   re-entry.

This must be peaceable. If the re-entry is blocked by the tenant, then the landlord has to initiate legal proceedings.

No act other than the above can constitute a valid act of forfeiture. In *Bank of Ireland v. Lady Lisa Ireland Ltd.* ([1993] I.L.R.M. 235) O'Hanlon J. held that the service of a notice which indicated that the lessor was exercising its right to determine the lease and demanding possession did not in itself constitute a sufficient act of forfeiture, unless combined with one of the above methods.

Even if the above grounds are satisfied, forfeiture may still be denied under the equitable remedy of relief against forfeiture, or by some statutory provision, for example under the Landlord and Tenant (Ground Rents) Act 1978 the landlord cannot forfeit for non-payment of rent if the tenant has the right to acquire the fee simple.

Ejectment for non-payment of rent

This is a statutory termination of a tenancy arising out of section 52 of Deasy's Act. It allows the landlord to initiate court proceedings to get the tenant out provided that:

(a)   a year's rent is due;

(b)   the tenancy is for a year or more (includes yearly tenancies but excludes weekly and monthly ones);

(c)   section 52 cannot be used in relation to a dwelling-house if the lessee has the right to the fee simple under the 1978 Act;

(d)   in special situations a remedy under section 52 may be denied.

The lessee can obtain a stay of the proceedings by producing rent. Even after proceedings have been completed and the lessee has been ejected, he may apply for an order of restitution He must do this within a period of six months. This means that the lessor cannot sell the premises for six months and consequently this makes section 52 quite ineffective. The alternative mechanism of forfeiture for breach of covenant is preferred by landlords.

Chapter 8

Licences and Estoppel

The distinction between personal and proprietary rights has been fundamental to the law on licences. A proprietary right is an interest over land which binds third parties. It may be sold or transferred by will. Some proprietary rights such as easements and the right to sue under restrictive covenants are annexed to land which is benefited by them and cannot be sold independently of the land. However, they can be transferred with the land.

A personal right, on the other hand, only exists as between two specific individuals. It is personal to those individuals. The person who has the right cannot transfer it to anyone else, and the right cannot bind third parties who purchase the land over which it has been granted.

A licence is a permission to occupy or exercise a right over land which is owned by somebody else. The person who is granted the right is known as the licensee. The owner of the land, the person who grants him the right is known as the licensor. A licence is generally understood to be a personal right. However, one development which casts a shadow on that assumption has been the appearance of a new category of licence known as the estoppel licence.

The equitable doctrine of proprietary estoppel has had a significant impact on land law. Its role in the Irish land law system has not yet been conclusively determined. It is discussed briefly in the second half of this chapter.

I: Types of Licences

Licence coupled with a proprietary interest

This is a licence granted in order to facilitate the exercise of an easement or profit. For instance, in order for a landowner to exercise his proprietary right to cut turf from a bog on his neighbour's land, he will need a concurrent licence to walk across the land to get to the bog. This licence will last as long as the incorporeal hereditament does. It binds all third parties who are bound by the incorporeal hereditament. However, it is very limited in scope since it only exists to facilitate the use of the easement or profit.

Bare licence

This is a licence which is not attached to any proprietary interest and has been given without consideration being received for it. It is a very weak form of licence and can be revoked by the grantor at any time on the giving of reasonable notice.

Contractual licence

This is a licence for which consideration has been given. Once consideration has been given, a contract between the licensee and licensor is regarded as being present, and the licence cannot be revoked by the licensor except in accordance with the terms of this contract. The court will grant an injunction to prevent its revocation by the licensor. However, a contractual licence does not bind third parties.

Originally the position was that as a licence was a personal right over land, the licensor could breach it with impunity. He could terminate the licence at any time and throw the licensee out and the licensee could do nothing to stop him. If the licensee had given consideration in return for the license, the licensee could sue the licensor for damages for breach of contract. That was the only remedy available to the contractual licensee.

The case of *Winter Garden Theatre (London) Ltd. v. Millennium Productions Ltd.* ([1948] A.C. 173) considerably increased the importance of contractual licences. This case established that, where a licensor attempted to throw a licensee off the land in breach of contract, the licensee could get an injunction to prevent the licensor from evicting him.

In the *Winter Garden* case the contract provided for a licence to hold plays and contracts in the defendant's theatre. It was held that the theatre owner could be stopped by injunction from revoking this licence in breach of contract. However, on the facts of the case the revocation was not in breach of contract.

Winter Garden had been anticipated in Ireland in *Whipp v. Mackey* ([1927] I.R. 372) which stated that an injunction could be granted to prevent a licensor from wrongfully revoking a licence.

However, these cases merely took a more generous approach to the remedies available for breach of personal rights. They did not convert licences from personal into proprietary rights. This view was conclusively reaffirmed by the House of Lords in *Ashburn Anstalt v. Arnold* ([1989] Ch. 1).

The House of Lords in *Ashburn* did indicate that a contractual licence might bind a third party in exceptional circumstances. However, it appears that such situations will be very limited as *Ashburn* made clear that even if the conveyance of land had been made expressly subject to the rights of the licensee, this would not be sufficient to justify the court in holding the purchaser bound by the licence.

Estoppel licence

This is a new and developing form of licence. It is a licence granted by a court in order to satisfy a proprietary estoppel. An estoppel licence may, if so directed by the court, bind third parties. It appears that the doctrine of proprietary estoppel may be utilised so as to create licences which actually bind third parties and are very close to proprietary rights.

II: Proprietary Estoppel

This is a doctrine whereby equity may take property rights away from somebody who has acted in an unconscionable manner and transfer them to the person who has suffered as a result of the unconscionability.

When can a claimant rely on the doctrine of estoppel?

Irish courts have recognised the concept of proprietary estoppel (most clearly in *McMahon v. Kerry Co. Council* ([1981] I.L.R.M. 419)), but have yet to lay down clear guidelines as to when it should apply. For the moment, those invoking estoppel in this jurisdiction will have to use as a template the conclusions from the United Kingdom and Commonwealth jurisprudence detailed below.

This jurisprudence has established that where one person incurs detriment in reliance on a belief that he has or will have an interest in land owned by another, the court may find that an estoppel has arisen. If the true owner of the land has encouraged this belief, or is aware of it and does not disabuse the mistaken person, he runs the risk of being estopped at a later date from pointing out that that person has no interest in the land.

An estoppel will not necessarily arise merely because the conditions in the above paragraph are satisfied. The overall principle is whether the true owner of land has acted unconscionably in the circumstances. The decision as to whether unconscionability is present depends to a large extent on the discretion of the judge.

At the moment there is a tendency to take a narrow view of unconscionability, as demonstrated by the recent United Kingdom decisions of *Taylor v. Dickens* ([1998] 1 F.L.R. 806) and *Gillett v. Holt* ([1998] 3 All E.R. 917).

Assuming estoppel is present, what remedies are available to the claimant?

When an estoppel exists, a court has a choice of remedies to give effect to it. It may order that the person who has suffered detriment should be paid compensation. It may grant him equitable ownership of the land under a constructive trust. Easements and leases have been granted where necessary to satisfy an estoppel. The court may even require the owner to convey the legal title in the land to the person who has incurred the detriment.

Another solution for the judge is to grant that person a licence over the land. Licences granted to satisfy an estoppel may, if directed, bind third parties. However, they are not full proprietary rights in so far as they cannot be transferred by the licensee.

The United Kingdom case of *Inwards v. Baker* ([1965] 2 Q.B. 29) is an example of a situation in which an estoppel licence binding third parties was granted by the courts. In this case a father suggested to a son that the son build a bungalow for himself on the father's land. On his death, the father left the land to his mistress. It was held that the father had given the son the belief that he could live on the land as long as he liked, and that the son had expended a considerable amount of money in building the bungalow in reliance on that belief. It was held that the son was entitled to remain on the land as long as he wished.

One Irish case in which an estoppel licence was granted is that of *Cullen v. Cullen* ([1962] I.R. 268). However, this judgment is a flawed one for a number of reasons. In particular the ground for granting the licence in that case was given as the contractual doctrine of promissory estoppel rather than the land law doctrine of proprietary estoppel. This error was replicated by the Irish courts in *Re J.R.* ([1993] I.L.R.M. 657). Thus, although *Cullen* is authority for the fact that Irish courts can grant an estoppel licence, it needs to be cited with reservation.

Chapter 9

Easements

An easement may be defined as a proprietary right which accrues to an individual by virtue of his ownership of land and which enables him to perform some act on the land of a neighbouring landowner which would otherwise constitute a trespass.

In total four characteristics are necessary for an easement to exist. First, because an easement is annexed to land, the person asserting the right must be able to show that he owns land in the neighbourhood of the land over which the right is exercised and that his land is benefited by the exercise of the right. In other words:

- There must be a dominant and a servient tenement.
- The dominant and servient tenements must not be owned and occupied by the same person.
- The easement must benefit the dominant tenement.
- The right must be capable of forming the subject-matter of a grant.

This has been summarised as meaning that it must be precisely defined and similar in nature to those rights historically established as easements.

I: CHARACTERISTICS OF AN EASEMENT

There must be a dominant and a servient tenement

As stated above, this follows logically from the fact that an easement is an incorporeal hereditament annexed to land.

For example, Alfred claims a right of way over Edith's land. Alfred must show that he has land in the vicinity of Edith's land which is benefited by the exercise of this right of way. Alfred's land is the dominant tenement; it gets the benefit of the alleged easement. Edith's land is the servient tenement; it bears the burden of the easement.

The dominant and servient tenements must not be owned *and* occupied by the same person

The word "and" in the above sentence is very important. It is not necessarily a bar to the recognition of an easement that the dominant and servient tenements are under common ownership, provided that they are occupied by different persons. For example, a tenant may acquire an easement against his landlord or against another tenant. This has been established in Ireland since the case of *Hanna v. Pollock* ([1900] 2 I.R. 664).

The easement must accommodate the dominant tenement

The easement must benefit the dominant tenement in some way. This means that it must benefit the owner in his capacity as landowner, rather than in a personal capacity. It must enhance his enjoyment of the dominant tenement.

In *Hill v. Tupper* ((1863) 2 H. & C. 121) the lessee of land adjoining a canal was granted the exclusive right by his neighbour, who owned the canal, to hire out pleasure boats on it. The issue was whether this right amounted to an easement or a licence. The court said that it was not an easement because the exclusive right to hire out pleasure boats on the canal was a commercial monopoly and, although it benefited the neighbouring owner as a businessman, it did not actually benefit him in the use of his riverbank land.

The merits of this decision have been much debated. At times it is difficult to draw the line between benefiting an individual in his use of land and benefiting him personally. It is important to remember that the courts are reluctant to recognise new easements which appear to fall harshly on the owner of the servient tenement. The right in this case was an exclusive one, and of a commercial nature. Recognising it would effectively deprive the owner of the servient tenement of the right to one of the potential sources of income from his property, *i.e.* the canal pleasure boat trade.

A contrasting case is that of *Moody v. Steggles* ((1879) 12 Ch.D. 261). Here it was held that the right of the owner of a public house to place a sign on adjoining premises advertising his business was capable of being an easement. The judge in this case felt that the right to advertise one's business on a neighbouring land was capable of enhancing one's use of the land.

Therefore, it should not be understood that a right which enhances a business carried on by the owner of the dominant tenement on his land is automatically incapable of qualifying as an easement. Instead it is worth using these cases to make the point that there is no clear-cut rule, in relation to new kinds of rights, as to whether they are capable of qualifying as easements or not.

What can be said is that the court will have considerations of justice in mind in answering this question and is unlikely to recognise rights as easements if they bear heavily on the owner of the servient tenement. Where the recognition of certain rights would lead to this problem, the courts will usually manage to exclude them by saying either that they do not benefit the dominant tenement or by saying that they are incapable of forming the subject-matter of a grant. Usually the latter mechanism is utilised, but in *Hill v. Tupper* it was the former one which was employed.

The right must be capable of forming the subject-matter of a grant

This requirement has two sub-components.

(a) The scope of the right must be precise and clear

The courts will not impose vague restrictions on the right to possession of the owner of the servient tenement. An example would be the reluctance to recognise a general "right to a view", which was displayed in *Dalton v. Angus & Co* ((1881) 6 App. Cas. 740). A widely recognised right to a view would seriously restrict building and, in addition to being questionable from the public policy point of view, would disproportionately restrict the development potential of the servient tenement.

(b) The right must be similar in nature to those rights historically recognised as easements

There are certain long established easements: the right to light; rights of way; and the right to support from an adjoining building. In *Dyce v. Hay* ((1852) 1 Macq. 305 at 312–313) Lord St. Leonards stated:

> "The category of servitudes and easements must alter and expand with the changes that take place in the circumstances of mankind."

Nonetheless, the courts subject new easements to careful scrutiny.

Copeland v. Greenhalf ([1952] Ch. 488) involved a wheelwright who was allowed by his neighbour to use part of his yard for repairing vehicles and to store some of the vehicles there. He argued that this right was an easement. This was rejected as the claimant was practically alleging a right to possession of part of his neighbour's property.

In the contrasting case of *Wright v. Macadam* ([1949] 2 K.B. 744) it was held that the right to exclusive use of a coal shed could constitute an easement. In *Middleton v. Clarence* ((1877) 11 I.R.C.L. 499) the right to throw spoil on a neighbour's land amounted to an easement.

The difficulty with recognising rights of storage and parking as capable of being easements is that this necessarily leads to an overlap between the rules on easements and the doctrine of adverse possession. Should an individual who stores property in a neighbour's shed be able to claim either a *de facto* title to the shed by adverse possession or, alternatively, an easement of storage, depending on which set of criteria suit him best?

This overlap is a very real possibility given that *Griffin v. Bleithin* ([1999] 2 I.L.R.M. 182) regarded the defendant's behaviour in storing property in a shed as demonstrating sufficient *animus possidendi* to extinguish the title of the original owner of the shed (see Chapter 15: Adverse Possession for further detail on this case).

In *Phipps v. Pears* ([1965] 1 Q.B. 76) it was held that there was no easement which guaranteed a building shelter from the wind and rain. In contrast with this case is the judgment of the Supreme Court in *Treacy v. Dublin Corporation* ([1993] 1 I.R. 305) the leading Irish case on the characteristics of an easement. In this case a right of protection from the weather was held to be necessary in order to ensure that an easement of support was observed. However, the right was dependent on the particular facts of the case and did not differ from *Phipps v. Pears* in this regard.

The "ancillary rights" doctrine put forward in *Treacy* is a method whereby rights not otherwise qualifying as easements can be raised to the status of easements by treating them as necessary for the enjoyment of other rights which exist and which are definitely categorised as easements. For example, it has yet to be conclusively decided in Ireland whether the right to park constitutes an easement or not. It has been argued that such a right should be recognised as an easement, at least where it is necessary for the enjoyment of established easements such as rights of way. In *Redfont Ltd. v. Custom House Dock Management Ltd.* (unreported, High Court, Shanley J., March 31, 1998) it was held on an interlocutory application that the plaintiffs had raised a fair issue to be tried as to whether an ancillary right to park cars was reasonably necessary to enjoy substantially certain rights of way granted to them as sub-tenants in the Irish Financial Services Centre.

The test that the courts are applying in this category has been described as an examination of whether the right is analogous to those historically listed as easements. As with the previous requirement that the easement benefit the dominant tenement, this test initially appears clear-cut but on closer examination may be a difficult question to decide. This is not helped by the fact that much of the case law cited above appears contradictory.

However, the cases are not as contradictory as they appear. In deciding whether to recognise new forms of easement most of the judgments are taking similar factors into account. The confusion arises because many judges avoid expressly mentioning these factors, preferring to operate them under cover of vague phrases such as "similar to those rights historically recognised as easements".

The key determining factors are as follows:

- The hardship that the recognition of such an easement is likely to cause to owners of servient tenements. A major sub-factor here is whether the alleged right compels the owner of the servient tenement to incur expenditure or perform positive duties.
- Public policy considerations, including the long-term consequences of the decision.
- Whether such a right is more appropriately achieved by use of other legal mechanisms such as restrictive covenants or licences.

II: Acquisition of Easements

If an easement is being claimed over someone else's property, it is not enough to show that the right asserted satisfies the characteristics of an easement. It must also be shown that the claimant acquired this right in some recognised way.

There are three main ways in which easements may be acquired:

- By express grant or reservation.
- By implied grant or reservation.
- By prescription.

As a preliminary point, it is necessary to outline the difference between a grant of an easement and a reservation of an easement. A reservation occurs where the vendor/lessor of land reserves an easement over the land sold/leased for the benefit of neighbouring land retained by him. A grant, on the other hand, usually occurs where the purchaser/lessee of land, in addition to getting the land he has purchased/leased, also gets easements over adjoining land which has been retained by the vendor/lessor. A grant of an easement (but not a reservation) may also occur independently of a sale of the dominant tenement.

Acquisition by express grant/reservation

This occurs when the grant or reservation is expressly stated in a document. The document may either be a document selling or leasing the dominant tenement or it may be an independent document designed specifically to transfer the easement in isolation.

Acquisition by implied grant/reservation

Implied easements are easements which are not granted expressly by the owner of the servient tenement but which are implied by the courts in situations where an individual sells or leases part of his land. Implied easements may either be implied grants, *i.e.* for the benefit of the part sold or implied reservations, *i.e.* for the benefit of the part retained.

Implied reservations

The courts do not like the idea of easements arising by reservation. Just as they construe express reservations strictly, so they are reluctant to imply reservations in a sale/lease for the benefit of the vendor/lessor. Until recently, the situations in which implied reservations could arise were thought to be very limited.

Traditionally, there were only two situations in which the courts were prepared to imply easements in a conveyance for the benefit of the vendor/lessor. The first was in the case of landlocked land: where the vendor/lessor had sold/leased all the land around the part retained and would have no legally enforceable way of entering or leaving his property if he were not granted a right of way over the part sold/leased. The courts have characterised this as an easement of necessity: it would be impossible for the owner of the dominant tenement to have any use of his property were the easement not granted.

The second situation arose in relation to the easement of support. Where an individual owns two houses with a common supporting wall and sells one of them, he is regarded as retaining an easement of support in relation to the house sold. In other words, the purchaser cannot demolish the house he has bought if to do so would mean the collapse of the vendor's house. This is explained as an easement of common intention: in situations where one of two adjoining houses is sold and the other retained by the vendor, it must be taken to be the intention of both parties to the conveyance that the purchaser should not demolish the house he has bought if to do so would cause the vendor's house to fall down.

However, the recent judgment of Kinlen J. in *Dwyer Nolan Developments Ltd. v. Kingscroft Developments Ltd.* ([1999] 1 I.L.R.M. 141) is indicative of an Irish trend towards expanding the circumstances in which reservations may be implied.

In *Dwyer Nolan* the plaintiff, a property developer, sold some of his land to the defendant, another property developer. This sale effectively left the land retained by the plaintiff landlocked, but at the time of the transfer the defendant had a grant of planning permission which provided for an access road from the plaintiff's property to the main road. The plaintiff intended to develop the retained land and the defendant knew of this intention.

However, subsequent to the transfer, the defendant got an alteration of the planning permission which abolished the access road from the plaintiff's property to the main road. The plaintiff still had some access in and out of his lands under the new planning permission, but by foot rather than by road. This made it impossible for the plaintiff to develop the land; however it was still possible for him to use it for agricultural purposes.

United Kingdom authority on the subject indicated that when a right of way of necessity arose in relation to landlocked land retained by a vendor, that right of way was limited to such access rights as were necessary for the purposes for which the land was being used at the time of the transfer. Although the plaintiff was entitled to a right of way, he was only entitled to a right of way for agricultural use, because that was the only use to which the land was being put at the time of the transfer.

However, Kinlen J. preferred to follow Irish authority to the contrary and, in so doing, adopted a much more relaxed attitude to the doctrine of easements of necessity. He stated that the retained land had always been understood by both parties to be development land intended for industrial use. The plaintiff was entitled to such right of way as was necessary for this use.

It is interesting to compare the judgment of Kinlen J. in *Dwyer Nolan* with the even more recent decision of the Court of Appeal in *Peckham v. Ellison* ([1999] Conv. 353). A local council sold off a council house to the defendant and retained a neighbouring house. They subsequently sold the neighbouring house to the plaintiff. The plaintiff claimed that a reservation in favour of the council was implied in the conveyance to the plaintiff. This easement would then have passed to the plaintiff when the council subsequently sold him the dominant tenement. The reservation alleged was a right of way for all purposes around the side and across the rear of the plaintiff's house.

It was held that the right of way in question had been reserved by implication in the conveyance to the defendant. It was necessary to imply this right to give effect to the common intention of the parties. Had the council and the defendant thought about it when the house was being sold, this easement would have been expressly reserved in favour of the council.

It may be seen that there is a growing trend on the part of both the United Kingdom and Irish courts to imply reservations into a conveyance. The correctness of such an approach is questionable and conflicts with traditional authority on easements. The broad approach taken to the concepts of necessity and common intention in the above cases may also result in an increase in the number of implied grants.

Implied grants

All implied grants are theoretically based on the intention of the parties to the land transfer. Therefore they may be rebutted by evidence of an express contrary intention in the document effecting the transfer. In addition the rules regarding implied grants of easements only come into operation if the land transfer is a voluntary one. No easements will be implied in a conveyance or lease which is involuntary, for example one required by statute.

The grounds on which grants are implied are as follows:

- Necessity.
- Common intention.
- The rule in *Wheeldon v. Burrows*.
- Section 6 of the Conveyancing Act 1881.

Necessity/Common intention   When land is purchased/leased, a grant of an easement may be implied over neighbouring land retained by the vendor/lessor either because of necessity or because it is regarded as being the common intention of the parties.

As outlined in the context of implied reservations, these concepts were interpreted narrowly. However, Kinlen J. in *Dwyer Nolan* expanded these concepts in order to imply a reservation of a secondary right of way into a conveyance.

In the context of implied grants, a similar attitude was demonstrated by the United Kingdom case of *Wong v. Beaumont Properties Trust Ltd.* ([1965] 1 Q.B.173). A lease of cellars specified that they be used as a restaurant. However, the ventilation system was inadequate, and in order for the health authorities to allow the property to continue as a restaurant, a new ventilation system would have to be installed which involved the fixing of a duct to property retained by the landlord. The landlord questioned the tenant's right to do this, but the court held that the tenant had an easement over the landlord's property to fix the ventilation system. This easement was characterised by the court as an easement of necessity; it was necessary if the property was to be used in the way specified as permissible. The parties must have intended such an easement to apply if necessary.

The court justified recognition of the easement in this case on the grounds of necessity but they also explained it in terms of the common intention of the parties. There appears to be a considerable amount of overlap between these two categories, and the court in *Wong* did not appear to see the need to draw any clear distinction between them.

The rule in *Wheeldon v. Burrows* ((1879) 12 Ch.D. 31)   This rule applies to elevate quasi-easements to the status of easements. Quasi-easements are rights which satisfy the third and fourth requirements for easements, in that they benefit the quasi-dominant land and are capable of being the subject-matter of a grant, but fail to qualify as easements because the dominant and servient tenements are owned and occupied by the same person. This is best illustrated by an example.

John owns two adjoining pieces of land, Blackacre and Whiteacre. His house is located on Whiteacre. Every day he exercises the right to walk from his house across Blackacre which is the quickest route to the local town. John's right to walk across Blackacre is of course not an easement as he owns and occupies both parcels of land and a landowner cannot have an easement over land which he already owns.

However, John's right of way over Blackacre is a quasi-easement in that it is a right which benefits him in his use of Whiteacre as a residence and a right of way is well established as a right which is capable of being the subject-matter of a grant. If John sold Whiteacre to Jill and retained Blackacre for himself, Jill might be able to employ the rule in *Wheeldon v. Burrows* to claim a right of way leading from her house, over Blackacre, to the local town.

The conditions for the application of the rule in *Wheeldon v. Burrows* are as follows:

(i)   The right claimed must have been in existence as a quasi-easement at the time of the purchase/lease of the dominant tenement.

This means that it must have been exercised by the common owner over the servient tenement for the benefit of the dominant tenement prior to the sale of the dominant tenement. In addition it must be a right which is capable of being the subject-matter of a grant.

(ii)   The right must be necessary for the reasonable enjoyment of the land granted.

This is not as strict as the necessity requirement which requires that the right must be necessary for any enjoyment of the land granted. The test here only requires the right to be necessary for reasonable enjoyment.

In *Borman v. Griffith* ([1930] 1 Ch. 493) this requirement was fulfilled. A secondary right of way over the servient tenement was granted under *Wheeldon v. Burrows*. Although there existed another right of way, the one which was sought was much more convenient; it led right up to the front door, and was the only suitable route for the heavy vehicles used by the lessee in his business. A useful contrast is the case of *Goldberg v. Edwards* ([1950] Ch. 247) where a lessee claimed a secondary route of access through the landlord's house. It was held that there was no right of access through the house under *Wheeldon v. Burrows*; previous occupiers had only used the outside passage.

(iii)   The right must be continuous and apparent.

The requirement that the easement be "continuous" does not mean that it needs to be incessant; rather that it should not have been exercised on a merely temporary basis. As regards the "apparent" requirement, this means that the right must have made some "obvious permanent mark" on the land, *i.e.* that its existence be capable of discovery on a reasonable inspection of the land. Examples would be pipes, a made road, or light flowing through windows. In *Hansford v. Jago* ([1921] 1 Ch. 322) a strip of land marked with tracks was held sufficient evidence to establish a right of way.

Section 6 of the Conveyancing Act 1881 Section 6 operates so as to imply easements in the following situation. Where there is a conveyance (as defined by the Act) of one of two adjoining plots of land which, prior to the conveyance, have been in common ownership but have had separate persons in possession of them, *e.g.* because one part was under a lease or a licence. Again, this is best illustrated by an example.

Alexander, the owner of two adjoining pieces of land, Blackacre and Whiteacre, leases Blackacre to Sheila and as a friendly act allows Sheila to store her turf in a shed on Whiteacre. Later Alexander either sells the fee simple to Sheila or renews her lease of Blackacre. Since a properly executed lease amounts to a conveyance under section 6, and since all the other conditions for the application of the section are satisfied, the effect of the lease is that a right to use the Whiteacre shed for the storage of turf becomes annexed to Blackacre.

The conditions necessary for section 6 to apply are as follows:

(i)   There must have been a conveyance as defined by the Act.

"Conveyance" is defined as including not only the transfer of the fee simple but also a mortgage or lease made by any instrument except a will. The effect of that definition is that neither an oral lease nor a contract for a lease is sufficient to bring section 6 into play. For example, *Borman v. Griffith* was a case where no lease had been validly executed. There was only a contract for a lease, and because of this section 6 could not apply.

(ii)   There must have been diversity of ownership and occupation prior to the conveyance.

There must have been a common owner of the dominant and servient tenements but the dominant tenement must have been occupied by someone else, either the purchaser/lessee under the conveyance in issue or a third party.

This criterion was imposed by *Long v. Gowlett* ([1923] 2 Ch. 177). It is vital to the application of section 6 and if it is not present the only recourse is to fall back on *Wheeldon v. Burrows*. Such diversity may be present where the conveyed land was previously held on a lease; the purchaser/lessee need not necessarily be the prior tenant. Another situation would be where someone was allowed to occupy the sold land as a licensee prior to the conveyance.

(iii)   The right must have been enjoyed by the occupier of the dominant tenement over the servient tenement prior to and up to the time of the conveyance.

If user stops before the execution of the conveyance because permission has been withdrawn by the common owner then section 6 cannot apply.

Acquisition by prescription

Express and implied easements have this in common: there must be some kind of land transfer from the owner of the servient tenement to the owner of the dominant tenement in order for them to exist. However, easements which arise by prescription are easements which are acquired by long user.

In order to acquire easements by prescription there are two main conditions which have to be fulfilled. First, it is necessary to show that the claimant or his predecessors in title have been in the habit of using the easement as if it belonged to them. Secondly, it must be that user of this kind has gone on for a specific period of time preceding the date of the court action.

Type of user

In order to acquire an easement by prescription (long user), the prima facie rule is that the user must have been without force, without secrecy and without permission. Permissive user merely creates a licence, not an easement by prescription.

However, the Prescription Act 1858 modifies the ban on permissive user to some extent. Permissive user may give rise to an easement by prescription if it has gone on for an extra-long period of time (40 years instead of the 20 years normally required for non-permissive user) and the user has not been enjoyed by written permission. An easement of light is acquired after only 20 years provided once again that it has not been enjoyed with written permission.

In the United Kingdom there is a requirement that the user be in fee simple, *i.e.* that it should have been by or on behalf of a fee simple owner against a fee simple owner. However, Irish courts have taken a different attitude. This is one area where Irish and English rules on prescription differ greatly.

Duration of user

This is specified in the Prescription (Ireland) Act 1858. The Act deals separately with easements of light and easements other than light.

As regards easements other than light, section 1 of the Act provides that such an easement is acquired after 20 years, provided that the user is the correct sort (not by permission, secrecy or fraud) and that it has continued up to the time of the court action. The Act also provides that the 20-year period must be uninterrupted, but that nothing counts as a statutory interruption unless it has been submitted to or acquiesced in by the dominant owner for one year after he had notice of the interruption and of the person responsible therefor.

The 20-year period does not apply to prescription against tenants or against their landlords. Thus, if the servient tenement is held on a tenancy, this section is inapplicable. You have to prove the longer period of user.

Periods during which the servient owner was an infant, lunatic or fee simple owner are deducted in calculating the 20-year period. These deductions do not count as interruptions and periods of user before and after the periods of disability may be added together to achieve the necessary 20 years.

Section 2 of the Act provides that after 40 years' user the claim shall be absolute and indefeasible unless it appears that it was enjoyed by some consent or agreement expressly given in writing.

One advantage of proving 40 years', as opposed to 20 years', user is that the claim cannot be defeated on the grounds that it was not of right because enjoyed by permission, provided of course that such permission was not in writing. Oral permission will not nullify a claim of 40-plus years, at least not if it was given before the commencement of the 40-year period.

There are no deductions in relation to periods of infancy, insanity or fee simple ownership if 40 years' user is shown.

Furthermore, you can prescribe against land held by a tenant under the 40-year period. Easements against the tenant can be successfully claimed after 40 years. If the lease has come to an end during your period of user and you want to claim prescription against the landlord then it is necessary to wait three years until after the end of the lease before bringing your claim. If the landlord fails to object within that period and you can show the requisite 40 years' user then your claim is safe.

If the landlord objects within the three years then the period during which the easement was held subject to a tenancy is deducted. The rule in relation to prescription against landlords is laid down by section 8 which in its terms only applies to rights of way and watercourses; however, this is understood to be a misprint and section 8 is widely understood as applying to all easements.

In respect of easements of light, user for more than 20 years automatically gives rise to an easement. The user in relation to easements of light may be by force, secrecy or permission so long as the permission is not in writing. Easements of light do not have to be of right so possibly may be obtained against a landlord while a tenancy is running.

Chapter 10

Freehold Covenants

Sometimes the owner of land enters into a deed with his neighbour in which he promises to refrain from carrying out some act on his land or, more rarely, to perform some act in relation to it. This often occurs when an individual purchases land and the vendor wants to protect adjoining land which he is retaining. The vendor requires the purchaser to enter into a freehold covenant with him as a condition of the sale. These covenants are known as freehold covenants, to distinguish them from covenants contained in leases. They represent a restriction on the freehold owner's right to freely use his land.

The person who has the right to sue on the covenant is known as the covenantee and the person who is bound by the restriction and liable to be sued if he breaches it is known as the covenantor.

Issues in relation to freehold covenants are twofold. It is clear that they bind the covenantor *vis-à-vis* the covenantee. Such is self-evident under ordinary principles of contract law. What is less clear is the extent to which they run with the land to bind successors in title of the covenantor and/or to empower successors in title of the covenantee to invoke them in court.

Thus, two principal questions arise regarding covenants entered into in relation to freehold land:

- First, assuming the original covenantee to have parted with his land, to what extent does the benefit of the covenant run with the land of the covenantee to allow it to be invoked by his successors in title?
- Secondly, assuming the original covenantor to have parted with his land, does the burden of the covenant run with the land of the covenantor so as to bind his successors in title?

It is traditional in land law exams to set problem questions on the topic of freehold covenants. There are four scenarios upon which the student may be required to advise. Take the following example:

A sells part of his land to B. As a condition of the transfer, B covenants not to put up any new buildings on the land he has purchased.

- Can A sue B if B breaches this covenant?
- If A sells his land on to C, can C invoke the covenant to stop B building on his land?
- Conversely, if A retains his land while B sells on his land to D, can A enforce the covenant against D?
- What if both A and B have parted with their land? Can A's successor in title, C, enforce the covenant against B's successor in title, D?

We will deal with each issue in turn.

Can the original covenantee sue the original covenantor for breach of a freehold covenant?

Problem scenario 1: A has retained his land. B has retained his land. Can A sue B?

The original covenantee can sue the original covenantor in contract, without having to rely on land law rules at all. Since A and B are the original parties to the covenant, A should have no difficulty in enforcing it against B.

However, if the original covenant is unenforceable under ordinary contract law principles, then of course it will not be possible for A to sue B. A recent Supreme Court case, *Sibra Building Co. Ltd. v. Ladgrove Stores Ltd.* ([1998] 2 I.R. 589) involved a consideration of whether a freehold covenant prohibiting the use of property as a pub or off-licence premises was in restraint of trade and in breach of the Competition Act 1991. The covenant had been entered into by the covenantor on the occasion of purchasing the property, and the vendor/covenantee owned a pub close by.

Both arguments were rejected. The doctrine of restraint of trade had never applied to invalidate freehold covenants. In addition, there could not be said to have been an "agreement between undertakings" for the purposes of the Competition Act 1991.

Can a successor in title of the original covenantee sue the original covenantor for breach of a freehold covenant?

Problem scenario 2: A has sold his land to C. B has retained

his land. Can C, a successor in title of the covenantee, sue B,
the original covenantor?

Provided that the following conditions are satisfied, a successor in
title of the covenantee can sue the original covenantor at common
law:

(a) The covenant must touch and concern the land of the covenantee. This means that the covenant must not be of personal benefit to the covenantee only. It must benefit him in
his capacity as landowner.

(b) The successor in title to the original covenantee must own a
legal estate in the land. The reason for this is that the common law does not normally recognise equitable interests in
land, and will not allow the common law rules to be used
to recognise benefits which are attached to an equitable estate.

(c) The successor in title to the original covenantee must possess the same type of estate as the original covenantee. The
consequence of this is that a tenant cannot enforce a freehold covenant entered into by his landlord. Also, a tenant in
tail or the holder of a life estate cannot enforce a covenant
entered into for the benefit of a fee simple predecessor in
title.

If a successor in title of the covenantee cannot bring himself within
the common law rules for passing of the benefit, he may neverthe-
less be able to make a case for passing of the benefit in equity. The
equitable requirements for passing of benefit are detailed later in
this chapter.

Can the original covenantee enforce the covenant against a successor in title of the original covenantor?

Problem scenario 3: A has kept his land but B has sold his.
Can A, the original covenantee, enforce the covenant against
a successor in title of the covenantor?

This raises the question of whether the right to sue under a freehold
covenant is a proprietary right which may be exercised by A over the
land to which it relates, irrespective of who owns that land.

The common law position

The common law position is that the burden of a freehold covenant cannot be tied to the land of the covenantor and will not be allowed to bind future owners of that land. There is one limited exception to this position, namely, the rule in *Halsall v. Brizell,* which is detailed immediately below.

However, the area of freehold covenants is one of the situations in which equity has intervened to modify the common law. Under the rule in *Tulk v. Moxhay* ((1848) 2 Ph. 774) the burden of a freehold covenant may run with the land in equity so that future owners of the covenantor's land are bound by it. This diverges from the common law view.

There is one exception to the rule that the burden does not run with the land at common law, which is the rule in *Halsall v. Brizell* ([1957] Ch. 169). This exception arises where there are mutual covenants conferring both a benefit and a burden on the people who entered into them. If the successor in title of one of the parties to the covenant is obtaining a benefit from other parties or their successors' observance of the covenants, he cannot claim that he is not bound by them.

In *Halsall v. Brizell,* the purchasers of plots within a housing estate all covenanted to contribute towards the maintenance of private roads and sewers. One of the original purchasers sold his property on to the defendant Brizell. B claimed that as he was not a party to the covenant he was not bound by it. He invoked the general common law rule that the burden did not pass with the land. However, the judge rejected this argument. He pointed out that Brizell, as a resident of the estate, benefited by his neighbours' observance of their covenants to repair and maintain. There is an ancient common law principle that persons cannot take the benefit under a deed without also accepting the obligation. Brizell could not take the benefit under a deed without also accepting the obligation himself. Therefore he was bound by the covenants even though he was not a party to them.

However, this exception only applies in a very limited set of circumstances. The covenantee who wants to enforce a freehold covenant against successors in title of the covenantor would be better advised to have recourse to the equitable principles on this matter.

The equitable doctrine of Tulk v. Moxhay

Under the rule in *Tulk v. Moxhay* ((1848) 2 Ph. 774) equity will regard successors in title of the covenantor as bound by the terms of the covenant if the following conditions are satisfied:

(a)   The covenant must be a negative or restrictive covenant. It must not impose positive obligations on the covenantor, but rather, must restrict him from doing something.

In *Rhone v. Stephens* ([1994] 2 A.C. 310) the roof of a house partly covered an adjoining property. The owner of the house had a covenant with his adjoining neighbour that he would keep the common roof tiled and water tight. The covenantor's property came into new hands. Could the covenant be enforced against the new owners? The House of Lords refused to enforce this covenant against the covenantor's successor in title because it was a covenant which carried positive obligations; the rule in *Tulk v. Moxhay* only applied to restrictive covenants.

In deciding whether a covenant is positive or negative the courts will look behind the language in which the covenant is framed to the substance of the obligation in question. For example, in *Tulk v. Moxhay* the covenant in question was expressed in positive language as involving a duty "to maintain the square as a garden". However, when one looked behind the wording to the substance of the obligation involved it became apparent that what was actually involved was a restrictive covenant prohibiting building.

(b)   The land to which the benefit of the covenant is attached must be in the vicinity of the burdened land and must be benefited by the covenant.

(c)   The right to sue a successor in title of the covenantor is an equitable proprietary interest. As such, we must decide whether the new owner should be bound by applying the general rules for deciding whether third party interests bind the transferee of land. These rules differ depending on whether the covenantor's land is registered or unregistered.

Unregistered land

The burden imposed by *Tulk v. Moxhay* is an equitable burden. As such, if existing over unregistered land, it can be extinguished by a sale of the legal estate in the land to a bona fide purchaser for value who has no actual or constructive notice of the covenant. Therefore, if the successor in title can show that he is the owner of the legal estate, that he gave consideration for the transfer, and that he had no actual, constructive or imputed notice of the covenant, he will not be bound by it.

Registered land
If the land burdened by the covenant is registered then a purchaser of that land will not be bound unless the covenant is marked on the Register as a burden. However, if the successor in title of the covenantor has received the land as a gift then he will be bound by the covenant whether it is marked on the Register or not.

[N.B. Students will find these rules discussed in greater detail in Chapter 11: Transfer of Land].

(d)   The rule in *Tulk v. Moxhay* may only be invoked by the original covenantee if he retains the land for the benefit of which the covenant was entered into.

There is one other requirement which we do not have to worry about in this situation as A is the original covenantee:

(e)   The rule in *Tulk v. Moxhay* may only be invoked by successors in title of the original covenantee if they can show that the benefit of the covenant has passed to them in equity. Showing passing of benefit at common law is not enough to justify appealing to the equitable rules on passing of burden and vice versa.

This requirement will be discussed in the next section of the chapter.

The facts of Tulk v. Moxhay
The facts of *Tulk v. Moxhay* were as follows: the plaintiff, Mr Tulk, sold a garden to E, requiring E to enter into a covenant to the effect that the land would be kept as a garden and not be covered by any buildings. E sold the land, and it passed through the hands of a number of people until it was purchased by the defendant, Mr Moxhay, who purchased it with notice of the covenant. Although Mr Moxhay knew of the covenant he tried to build on the land. Mr Tulk brought an action to stop him on the ground that he was in breach of covenant. Mr Moxhay argued that he was not bound by the covenant. He cited the common law rule that the burden does not pass to successors in title of the covenantor.

It was held that an injunction could be granted in equity against Mr Moxhay restraining him from breaching the restrictive covenant. The burden of a restrictive covenant ran with the land in equity. Conditions (a)–(d) above were satisfied. The covenant was a restrictive one and Mr Moxhay had had notice of it. In addition, Mr Tulk, the original covenantee, had retained land in the vicinity of the square which was benefited by the covenant. As a continuing householder in the area, it was in his interest to see that the land was not built up.

Can a successor in title of the original covenantee enforce the covenant against a successor in title of the original covenantor?

Problem scenario 4: A has sold his land to C and B has sold his land to D. C wants to enforce the covenant against D. Can a successor in title of the original covenantee sue a successor in title of the original covenantor?

As we have seen, a successor in title of the original covenantor may be sued under *Tulk v. Moxhay* in equity but all the necessary constituents of this rule must be satisfied.

In particular condition (e) in *Tulk v. Moxhay*, which was briefly mentioned above, assumes great importance in this scenario.

Condition (e) states that, if the person trying to invoke *Tulk v. Moxhay* is not the original covenantee but a successor in title, then he must show that the benefit of the covenant has passed to him in equity. This can be quite a difficult condition to fulfil as the benefit does not pass as easily in equity as at common law.

The benefit of the covenant will only pass in equity if:

(a)   the covenant touches and concerns the land of the covenantee;

(b)   the land owned by the covenantee is now owned by the applicant; and

(c)   one of the following three conditions is satisfied:
   (i)   The benefit of the covenant was annexed to the land.
   (ii)   The benefit of the covenant was assigned with the land.
   (iii) The land benefited and the land burdened were part of a scheme of development.

The first two conditions are straightforward. However, there is a lot of case law on the various components of condition (c). Remember that only one of these components need be fulfilled in order for the benefit to pass in equity. We will now go on to look at each of the components in turn.

Annexation

This requires that at the time the covenant was created, both parties to the covenant intended that the benefit of the covenant should run with the land, *i.e.* that the covenant could be invoked by successors in title of the covenantee. This intention is evident where the covenant states that it is made for the benefit of the land or that it is made with the covenantee in his capacity as landowner. Both statements are regarded as demonstrating an intention that future owners of the land should have the benefit of the covenant.

For example, in *Rogers v. Hosegood* ([1900] 2 Ch. 388) a restrictive covenant was held to be annexed to the land of the covenantee because it was stated to be in favour of the vendors of certain land, their assigns and others claiming under them, for the benefit of adjoining land.

The scope of the property to which the covenant is to be annexed must be clearly defined. This was not the case in *Renals v. Cowlishaw* ((1878) 9 Ch. D. 125) where a claim of annexation failed for this reason.

In addition, the property described as property to which the covenant is annexed should be property which is touched and concerned by the covenant, otherwise the annexation may be struck down as too wide.

In *Re Ballard's Conveyance* ([1937] Ch. 473) the benefit of the covenant was annexed to an estate of 1700 acres. Only a small part of this land was capable of being benefited by the covenant. It was held that the covenant was not enforceable by the purchasers of the estate.

One unresolved issue relates to the possibility of statutory annexation of all covenants of freehold land so that their benefit automatically runs with the land in equity. Section 58 of the Conveyancing Act 1881 provides as follows: "A freehold covenant shall be deemed to be made with the covenantee and his heirs and assigns". It has been argued that this provision has the effect of annexing all freehold covenants to the covenantee's land in equity so that the benefit of them automatically runs with the land. However, the balance of academic authority is against the statutory annexation argument.

Assignment

When the covenant is not annexed to the land so as to run automatically with it, there is still a possibility that the benefit may run with the land if it is passed on expressly in every assignment of that land.

The assignment of the covenant must be contemporaneous with the assignment of the land. Hence, once the land has been sold the covenant cannot be subsequently assigned.

However, what happens if the covenant benefits a particular area of land and part of the land from that area is sold off without the benefit being transferred? Given that land is retained which is benefited by the covenant, can the covenant be later transferred to the purchaser? *Re Union of London and Smith's Bank Ltd.'s Conveyance* ([1933] Ch. 611) answers this question in the negative.

Scheme of development

This is a peculiar doctrine of equity used to control housing estates and developments. The objective of many estate planners is that each house in the estate should be subject to similar restrictive covenants, in order to ensure the correct appearance and maintenance of the estate. The aim of the estate planners is that each house in the estate should be bound by these covenants and that the householder should also be able to enforce them against other owners of houses in the estate. In such a situation equity will recognise a passing of the burden without looking for annexation or assignment.

The original way of achieving mutual benefit and burden consisted of arranging for the sale of all the houses on the estate to be sold at the one time and for the purchasers to enter into a deed of mutual covenant at the time of sale. However, in most cases, houses on an estate would not all be sold at the same time.

Therefore, equity developed a more pragmatic solution. Equity provides that the purchaser of a house in a "scheme of development" only needs to covenant with the vendor. Even though there is no actual agreement with owners of houses which have been previously sold, equity regards these as being within the benefit of the covenant. Everyone living within the scheme of development can enforce these covenants against anyone else living within the scheme.

Hence, basically, the benefit automatically runs with the land in equity if the property in question is part of a scheme of development. A scheme of development occurs where there is a development within a clearly defined area, with all property holders within the area intended to be subject to a framework of mutual rights and obligations. The purchasers of property within the development must be aware of the scope of the development, and the particular rights and obligations attached to it.

It is difficult to explain the rationale behind this doctrine, and it has been remarked that it may be one of those branches of equity which works best when explained least.

In order for the reciprocal obligations and rights to apply the following conditions must be fulfilled:

1. The same vendor must have owned all the land subject to the scheme originally.
2. Before selling the land the vendor must have divided the land into lots subject to common restrictions.

This requirement is not applied strictly, as is shown by the case *of Baxter v. Four Oaks Properties Ltd.* ([1965] Ch. 816) and *Re Dolphin's Conveyance* ([1970] Ch. 654).

3. The restrictions must be of benefit to all the lots.
4. There must be disclosure of the nature and terms of the scheme to individual purchasers. They must know that the rights and obligations are reciprocal and they must know their content.
5. The area within which the scheme operates must be definite and known to the participants. Otherwise they will not be aware of the scope of their rights and obligations.

In conclusion, the fourth problem scenario is the most complicated to advise on and this, presumably, is why it is a favourite with examiners. To summarise the law on this issue, a successor in title of the covenantee may sue a successor in title of the covenantor under *Tulk v. Moxhay*, provided that he can satisfy the first four conditions in *Tulk v. Moxhay* and also show that the benefit has passed to him in equity either by annexation, assignment or under the scheme of development principle.

It is worth noting whether the situation comes within the *Halsall v. Brizell* common law exception to passing of burden, because, if it does, then a successor in title of the original covenantee may sue a successor in title of the original covenantor at common law without having to concern himself with the more stringent equitable requirements for passing of benefit. But the situations in which *Halsall v. Brizell* would apply are very rare.

Chapter 11

Transfer of Registered and Unregistered Land

Transfer of land may take place *inter vivos* or on death. An *inter vivos* transfer is a transfer of land from a living person. An *inter vivos* transfer takes place by a deed of conveyance transferring the land to the new owner. In the case of registered land the transfer is only complete when the transferee has been entered on the Land Register as the new owner of the land.

An *inter vivos* conveyance may be a gift or a sale, depending on whether consideration has been given for the transfer. A transfer of land on death takes place under a will or, if no valid will exists, according to the rules of intestacy. This chapter concentrates on *inter vivos* transfers or, as they are alternatively described, conveyances. The procedure for the transfer of land and other property on death is dealt with in Chapter 14: Succession Law.

In relation to any *inter vivos* transfer of either registered or unregistered land, it is vital to consider the Family Home Protection Act 1976. This Act applies where the present owner of the property is married, and the property to be sold is presently a family home. The failure of the non-owning spouse to give her written consent to the transfer may render it void. See below Chapter 12: The Family Home Protection Act. It is advised that students additionally read that chapter in order to gain a full understanding of the land transfer process.

It has already been mentioned that certain words of limitation have to be used in order for the fee simple estate in unregistered land to be transferred *inter vivos*. However, words of limitation do not have to be used in a deed of conveyance which transfers the fee simple estate in registered land. The Registration of Title Act 1964 has greatly simplified the transfer of registered land, although there still remain certain pitfalls for the purchaser. In relation to unregistered land, however, conveyancing is a more complicated affair.

Prior to a sale of land taking place it is important that the prospective purchaser find out what exactly he is buying.

He needs to find out:

- whether the person selling has a fee simple estate; and
- whether there are any third party interests (easements, covenants, trusts, estoppels, etc.) burdening the land.

This process is known as investigation of title. The task of investigation of title differs as between registered and unregistered land.

I: Investigation of Title to Unregistered Land

Determining whether the vendor has a fee simple estate

The transferee must make investigation of title to check that the transferor actually has the interest which he is purporting to transfer. In theory, it is necessary for the vendor to deduce title back for 40 years (although 20 years is often accepted as sufficient in practice).

The vendor has first to show a good root of title which dates from at least 40 years ago. A good root of title basically means a deed conveying the fee simple estate in the relevant land. In addition, the vendor will have to trace an unbroken chain of title from the root of title right up to the document giving him ownership of the land.

Identifying third party interests

Even when good title is shown the purchaser needs to concern himself with the possibility of third parties having interests in the land.

Examples of potential third party interests are as follows:

- Easements.
- *Profits à prendre.*
- Covenants.
- Estoppel rights.
- Rights under an express trust.
- Rights under an implied trust.

Looking at the above list, easements and profits are legal third party interests. The others are equitable third party interests and therefore weaker in one respect.

A purchaser of unregistered land is bound automatically by all legal third party interests. Normally he is bound by any equitable third party interests as well.

However, in one limited situation he can take free of equitable third party interests, provided that he can satisfy the following two requirements:

(a)　He must show himself to be the purchaser of the legal estate without notice of the interests.

(b)　The equitable interests must not be contained in a document which has been registered in the Registry of Deeds.

(a) The purchaser of the legal estate without notice

As explained briefly in Chapter 1, this individual is known as *"equity's darling"* because equity does not consider that he should be bound by equitable interests.

In order to qualify as equity's darling a transferee must be a purchaser. An individual who receives property under a will or as a gift can never qualify.

Secondly, the transferee must have purchased the legal estate in the property. A transferee who merely obtains equitable ownership of the property by purchasing the interest of a beneficiary under a trust is bound by all other equitable interests attaching to the property.

Thirdly, and most importantly, the transferee must have no notice of the equitable interests. This means that he must have no actual or constructive knowledge of their existence. Even if the transferee did not actually know of the existence of the interests at the time he purchased the property, he may still be bound by them. A purchaser is regarded as having constructive notice of all interests which would have been evident to a purchaser taking reasonable care and making reasonable inquiries. The standard of care in this respect is quite high. The negligent purchaser can never be equity's darling.

Moreover, the concept of notice extends beyond actual or constructive knowledge in two respects. First, it includes the concept of imputed notice. A purchaser is held responsible for the actual or constructive knowledge of his solicitor. This is of particular concern to the purchaser, since a solicitor, being a professional in conveyancing transactions, has to keep to a very high standard of care in order to avoid being fixed with constructive knowledge.

In addition, the doctrine of notice incorporates the extremely significant rule in *Hunt v. Luck* ([1902] 1 Ch. 428). This case laid down the principle that a purchaser is automatically regarded as having constructive notice of the rights of everyone living on the property at the time of the sale. The one exception is if the purchaser has actually asked the relevant occupiers about their rights and they have denied that they have any. In that circumstance he is held entitled to take them at their word.

All in all, it may be quite difficult for a purchaser to show that he has had no notice of equitable interests attaching to the land. Even if he does manage to surmount this hurdle, he still has to consider the possibility that the equitable interests may have been contained in a document which has been registered in the Registry of Deeds.

(b) The Registry of Deeds

The Registry of Deeds system modifies the doctrine of notice. If any of the equitable interests in question were granted in a written document, and this document has been registered in the Registry of Deeds, they will bind even the purchaser of the legal estate without notice. It is necessary for prospective purchasers to make very careful searches in the Registry of Deeds. Such searches are time-consuming and expensive.

It can be seen that transfer of unregistered land is a hazardous process for the purchaser. Even when he has studied the title deeds produced to him and ascertained that the vendor has a good fee simple estate, he may find himself bound by legal or equitable third party interests.

II: INVESTIGATION OF TITLE TO REGISTERED LAND

The introduction of registered land was designed to simplify conveyancing and to get rid of the many complications which ensue in the course of conveying unregistered land. The policy behind the registered land system was twofold: it aimed both to excuse the vendor from the duty of having to deduce title and to relieve the purchaser from the duty of having to investigate it. The law governing our registered land system is currently contained in the Registration of Title Act 1964, and the statutory instruments passed thereunder.

The thinking behind the introduction of a system of registered land was that prospective purchasers should merely have to check the

Register of Title in order to discover the interests which existed in relation to the land. If interests existed which were not referred to on the Register, the purchaser would not be bound by them.

At this point the Registration of Title system appears to be a purchaser's Utopia. He merely has to consult the Register. However, the doctrine of overriding interests contained in section 72 of the 1964 Act represents the fly in the ointment so far as the purchaser of registered land is concerned.

Overriding interests are listed in section 72(1) of the Registration of Title Act 1964, and do not have to be registered. They bind purchasers automatically, whether or not they are recorded on the Register. The list of interests in section 72(1) includes leases for less than 21 years, as well as squatters' rights, and certain easements.

The most important overriding interest is contained in section 72(1)(j), namely, "the rights of any person in actual occupation of the land" at the time of the sale. There are a number of cases on the interpretation of this subsection, which need to be known in detail.

However, in one respect at least the registered land system makes investigation of title considerably easier. There is no longer a need for deduction of title documents in order to identify whether the vendor has a fee simple estate. This can be ascertained merely by consulting the Register.

Determining whether the vendor has a fee simple estate

In respect of registered land, particular individuals are recorded on the appropriate Register as being owners of the freehold interest, of the leasehold interest or of rentcharges, if any, which exist in relation to that land.

Sometimes an occupier of land might seek to register their freehold or leasehold interest in land but the validity of their claim might be in doubt. There is provision for the Registrar to give them a non-absolute title until such time as they can prove their title conclusively.

The classes of title recorded on the Register are as follows:

- Absolute title.
- Qualified title.

If an applicant for registration had difficulty in proving title, the Registrar would put him into this latter class. The entry on the Register would contain a provision outlining the particular flaws in title. For example, in relation to a particular qualified title, the Registrar might enter a note saying that, as this title could only be shown since 1960, the title granted by him is subject to any rights arising before 1960.

- Possessory title.

This title would be granted to a squatter who had been in adverse possession of land for less than the 12-year limitation period. Once the squatter gets over the 12 years he can have a qualified title saying that he has rights against the dispossessed owner and all persons claiming through the dispossessed owner but not against persons claiming through another source.

- Good leasehold title.

A good leasehold title gives a tenant a title to the leasehold interest in property, but it expressly states that it does not affect the right of any person which conflicts with the right of the lessor. This form of title would be used to designate a leasehold owner in a situation where the tenant's lease was valid but the landlord had some problem in showing his title to the land.

The phrase "converting titles" refers to the practice of moving a title out of one class and into another, *e.g.* raising a squatter's possessory title up to a qualified title after he has shown 12 years' adverse possession. This can be done on the application of an interested party or, alternatively, by the Registrar on his own initiative.

Identifying third party interests

Third party interests in registered land are divided into:

(a)   Minor interests.
(b)   Overriding interests.

(a) Minor interests

Minor interests are third party interests which are entitled to be recorded on the Register. If minor interests are registered, they bind all transferees of the land. If minor interests are unregistered, purchasers take free of them, but they still bind individuals who receive the land as a gift. The first thing that a purchaser of registered land ought to do is to check the Register to see which minor interests are recorded on it.

Minor interests are also described as registrable burdens. A list of these interests is provided in section 69(1) of the Registration of Title Act 1964. The most important minor interests are as follows:

- A charge on the land created after first registration.
- A rentcharge or fee farm or other perpetual rent.
- A vendor's lien on the land for unpaid purchase money.
- A lease for more than 21 years (this must not only be registered as a burden on the freehold Register but also requires registration in its own right on the leasehold Register).
- A judgment or order of a court, *e.g.* property adjustment orders.
- A judgment mortgage.
- Any easement or profit created by express grant after first registration.
- All freehold covenants.
- Rights of residence.
- A power of distress or entry.

(b) Overriding interests

In contrast to minor interests, checking the Register will not provide a purchaser with immunity from overriding interests. As already stated, these are interests which bind the purchaser without the need for registration. They are listed in section 72(1) of the Act as follows:

- Any estate duty, farm tax, gift tax and inheritance tax.
- Any annuities or rentcharges under the Land Purchase Acts.
- All public rights of way.
- All customary rights.
- Any easements and profits other than those created by express grant or reservation after first registration.
- Leases of less than 21 years.
- Rights acquired or in the course of being acquired under the Statute of Limitations 1957.
- The rights of every person in actual occupation of the land or in receipt of the rents and profits thereof save where inquiry is made of such person and the rights are not disclosed (subsection (1)(j)).

Further detail on section 72(1)(j)

"Rights"

First, subsection (1)(j)) only applies where the person in actual occupation has "rights" in relation to the land.

National Provincial Bank v. Ainsworth ([1965] A.C. 1175) stated that the word "rights" under the United Kingdom equivalent of section 72(1)(j) referred to proprietary rights and did not include personal rights such as rights under a licence or under the Family Home Protection Act. *Ainsworth* was followed in Ireland by *Guckian v. Brennan* ([1981] I.R. 478) in which it was held that a wife's rights under the Family Home Protection Act were personal rights only and could not constitute overriding interests. In *Webb v. Pollmount Ltd* ([1966] Ch. 584) it was stated that an option to purchase land was a proprietary right and could constitute an overriding interest.

"Actual occupation"

The second condition for subsection (1)(j) is that the person who has the rights must be in actual occupation of the land at the time of the sale. There are a number of cases detailing what constitutes actual occupation.

In *Williams & Glyns Bank v. Boland* ([1981] A.C. 487) a wife had an interest in the family home under a constructive trust. She was living there with her husband. It was held that she was in actual occupation for the purposes of the subsection. A wife did not have to have sole possession to come under section 72(1)(j). Joint possession with her husband was sufficient.

In *Kingsnorth Finance v. Tizard* ([1996] 1 W.L.R. 783) a wife invoked the United Kingdom equivalent of the subsection. She was sleeping elsewhere but came in every day to clean and care for the children. She had also left most of her belongings in the house. It was held that she too was in actual occupation.

In *Wallcite Ltd. v. Ferrishurst Ltd.* ([1999] 1 All E.R. 977) it was held that it is not necessary for the person in actual occupation to be in occupation of the whole of the land over which his interest subsists; it is sufficient if he is in actual occupation of a part of it at the time of the sale. This will cause the interest to bind the purchaser even in respect of the unoccupied part. The result of the decision is that an individual who wishes to purchase part of registered land should not only make inquiries about the rights of people living on the part he is actually purchasing, but should also inquire of all the individuals living on any part of the registered land whether they have rights which attach to the part he is purchasing.

In conclusion, purchasers of registered land are not bound by minor interests which have not been registered. They are bound by overriding interests and by registered minor interests whether they have notice of them or not. The doctrine of notice does not apply to registered land.

Individuals who receive registered land as a gift are bound by all third party interests over the land. The same position exists in relation to unregistered land.

III: ADDITIONAL DETAIL ABOUT THE REGISTRATION OF TITLE SYSTEM

What land is registered land?

Much registered land was registered because its registration was made compulsory. The Minister for Justice is entitled to make an order designating a particular county as a compulsory registration area. Once this is done, whenever there is a conveyance of any land within the designated area, that land must be registered by the new owner in order for his title to be valid. This applies whether the conveyance is one of a freehold or a leasehold interest. So far only one order has been made by the Minister under this provision. He has designated Counties Carlow, Laois and Meath as compulsory registration areas from January 1, 1970.

What happens if registration is compulsory and no one registers it? If someone is obliged to register, and he fails to do so on the relevant date (within six months after the conveyance), he loses his title to the land.

However, quite apart from compulsory registration, any owner of unregistered land can apply to the Land Registry to be put on the Register. Once his title has been registered the land becomes registered land and cannot subsequently be taken off the Register.

Administration of the Registration of Title system

The Registration of Title system is administered by the Land Registry and managed and controlled by the Registrar of Titles.

There are three distinct Registers kept in relation to each piece of registered land:

(a)   Register of ownership of freehold land.
(b)   Register of ownership of leasehold interests (only leasehold interests with at least 21 years left to run may be registered on this register).
(c)   Register of incorporeal hereditaments in gross. This does not apply to easements because they are not hereditaments in gross but includes profits and rentcharges.

Each of the three Registers is contained in a folio which is further divided into three parts.

Part 1 contains a description of the land, making reference to the precise location of the land on the Land Registry Map. It sets out the boundaries of the land.

Part 2 contains the name and address of the person or persons currently entitled to the freehold interest, leasehold interest or incorporeal hereditaments, depending on the particular Register.

Part 3 lists any charges and mortgages over the land, along with any burdens which may be registered as registered burdens, *e.g.* easements, restrictive covenants.

Rectification of the Register

Section 32 of the Registration of Title Act 1964 provides for rectification of errors in the Land Registry files. The Registrar may rectify the error, but he must first obtain the consent of the registered owner. If he fails to get this consent, he may apply to court for an order allowing rectification. The court will grant this order if it feels that such rectification may be carried out without injustice.

Chapter 12

Spousal Rights under the Family Home Protection Act

The Family Home Protection Act 1976 states that the family home cannot be conveyed by a spouse without the consent of the other spouse. The consent of the non-owning spouse is required in all cases, even when that spouse owns no interest at all, legal or equitable, in the family home. If the consent is not obtained, the transfer is void, unless it is to a *purchaser for full value*. A purchaser for full value is defined by the Act as a person who in good faith purchases an interest in property. The burden of proof is on the purchaser to show that this term applies to him.

There are provisions in the Act defining the concepts of "conveyance", "consent" and "family home" as well as provisions dispensing with the spouse's consent.

The Family Home Protection Act only applies to married couples and not to couples who are living together.

Moreover, it only confers personal rights, not proprietary rights, on the spouse. This was established by *Guckian v. Brennan* ([1981] I.R. 478).

The Family Home Protection Act 1976 is very important for conveyancers. Every transfer or creation of interest in land must be checked to see, first, if it comes within the Act, and, secondly, if the necessary consent has been obtained. For this reason, it often appears on exams. Although it may often only feature as part of a problem question, an examiner might fail a student for missing this point.

Whenever the student or practitioner is faced with a situation involving a mortgage, lease or sale of land, it is necessary to consider, first, whether this land is a family home. If it is, it is important to know whether the written consent of the vendor's spouse has been obtained to the transfer.

I: DEFINITIONS IN THE FAMILY HOME PROTECTION ACT

Conveyance

A conveyance is defined as including a mortgage, lease, and any disposition of an interest in property other than by will. It includes a contract to create any of the above. Case law has established that a transfer by operation of law, such as a judgment mortgage or possibly an estoppel, would not require spousal consent.

Family home

This is defined as a dwelling where the non-owning spouse ordinarily resides or has so resided before leaving the other spouse. Any building occupied as a separate dwelling constitutes a family home. The definition also includes all land ancillary to the dwelling. A house on a farm may be a family home, but the farmland itself would not be covered by the definition. It appears that if the conveyance is one which transfers both the farm and the house, it may be severed by the court so as to be void in so far as it relates to the house and valid in so far as it relates to the other property. A mobile home may constitute a dwelling.

Prior consent in writing

The consent must be in writing and executed before the conveyance takes place. However, the courts have been flexible in interpreting this requirement. In *Bank of Ireland v. Hanrahan* (unreported, High Court, February 10, 1987) the consent was given two hours after an equitable mortgage had been completed by the husband handing over the title deeds to the bank. The court held that there was an implied condition in the transfer of the title deeds that the bank would merely hold them for safekeeping and not for security for the loan until the wife's consent was completed.

The Family Law Act 1995 provides that a spouse may make a general and open-ended consent in writing to future transfers of the family home. Once she signs such a document her consent to future transfers will no longer be necessary. This provision has been criticised on the ground that it allows couples to opt out of the Act.

However, it is important to note that any consent under the Acts must be voluntary. It cannot be obtained by undue influence, duress, misrepresentation or mistake. It must be an informed consent. The spouse must appreciate the consequences of what she is signing. This has been demonstrated by *Bank of Ireland v. Smyth* ([1993] 2 I.R. 102) and *Allied Irish Banks v. Finnegan* ([1996] 1 I.L.R.M. 401) (discussed below). It is suggested that the courts will be particularly vigilant to ensure that a general consent under the Family Law Act 1995 is a fully informed consent.

II: EXCEPTIONS TO THE REQUIREMENT OF CONSENT

Sale by co-owning spouses

Where the spouses are co-owners and parties to the sale, consent is not required from either of them. This was established by the case of *Nestor v. Murphy* ([1979] I.R. 326) in which it was held that the purpose of the Act did not require consent in such cases. Obviously, both spouses had consented to the sale in that situation, even though they might not have complied with the formal requirements of the Act regarding consent.

General consent under the Family Home Protection Act 1995

This has been discussed above.

Consent to contract of sale

Where a spouse has made an informed consent in writing to a contract of sale, there is no need for her to make another consent to the conveyance carrying out that contract.

Conveyance to the non-owning spouse

There is no need for a spouse to consent to a conveyance which is in her favour.

Conveyance subject to an agreement entered into with a third party before marriage

Because the obligation to convey was entered into before marriage, there is no need for the other spouse to consent.

Conveyances to a purchaser for full value

This is the most important exception. The Act states that a conveyance will not be void if it was made in favour of a purchaser for full value and defines a purchaser as someone who in good faith acquires an interest in property. *Somers v. Weir* ([1979] I.R. 94) held that this provision incorporated the equitable doctrine of notice into the Family Home Protection Act. A purchaser cannot be a purchaser in good faith if he has actual, constructive or imputed notice of the fact that consent ought to have been and/or has not been obtained (see above Chapter 11: Transfer of Registered and Unregistered Land for an outline of the concept of notice).

In *Bank of Ireland v. Smyth* ([1993] 2 I.R. 102) a purchaser was held to be fixed with constructive notice of the fact that a spouse's consent was invalid. The reason for the consent being invalid was that the spouse did not fully appreciate the implications of the document she was signing. It was held that the bank had constructive notice of the fact that the consent was invalid. Had they acted as a reasonable purchaser would have done they would have made inquiries into the wife's understanding of the transaction and discovered that she was not fully informed.

In *Allied Irish Banks plc. v. Finnegan* ([1996] 1 I.L.R.M. 401) it was held that the onus of disproving actual or constructive knowledge lay on the individual or institution seeking to avail of the purchaser for value exception. This is a heavy burden to fulfil, given the known difficulties which attach to proving a negative fact.

Situations where consent can be dispensed with

Section 4 of the Act makes provision for dispensing with a spouse's consent:

- where the non-disposing spouse has deserted;
- where there is unsoundness of mind or mental disability on the part of the non-disposing spouse;
- where the non-disposing spouse cannot be found;
- where it is unreasonable for a spouse to withhold consent.

Hamilton v. Hamilton ([1982] I.R. 466) establishes guidelines for deciding whether a refusal to consent is unreasonable. The court may take into account the relative financial positions of the parties, in addition to any emotional disturbance which may be caused to the spouse and/or the children by the trauma of having to leave the family home. It was emphasised that it is important to take both parties' points of view into account when deciding the question of reasonableness.

Chapter 13

Mortgages

A mortgage occurs where the legal or equitable title to an interest in land is transferred as security for a loan, one of the conditions for the transfer being that if the loan is repaid on the due date, the mortgagor will get his title back. The land transfer provides the lender with security for the loan. It gives him priority over other creditors of the borrower.

There are two parties to a mortgage: the mortgagor and the mortgagee. It is very important for exam purposes to distinguish between them. The mortgagor is the person who borrows the money and gives up his property in consequence. The mortgagee is the person or institution which lends the money and gets an interest in the property as security for their loan. Hence, if John buys a house, and borrows the money from the bank to do so, the bank will usually require a mortgage over John's house until the money is repaid. John will be the mortgagor, and the bank will be the mortgagee.

A mortgage is in effect a transfer of property subject to a condition subsequent. However, equity and statute have stepped in to modify the law of mortgages to some extent so that transfer by mortgage is a *sui generis* category of transfer (a type of land transfer where special rules apply) and for this reason it is dealt with separately in this book.

The first modification occurred with equity's recognition of what was known as the equity of redemption.

Under the old law, a mortgage involved a transfer of property to the mortgagee which was liable to be terminated on a condition, *i.e.* the mortgagor repaying on the due date. If the mortgagor did not repay on the due date the mortgagee could keep the property forever. However, this changed when the courts of chancery recognised the concept of the equity of redemption. According to this doctrine, the mortgagee had the right to redeem at any time, even after the due date had passed. This could not be taken away by clauses in the mortgage agreement.

Under the equity of redemption, the only way that the mortgagor's right to get his property back on repayment can be lost is if foreclosure or sale has taken place. It is well to remember that every mortgage is in fact a transfer of an interest in land from the mortgagor to the mortgagee, albeit one hemmed in by equitable rules. One aspect of the old law that still survives is the mortgagee's right to possession, although he will commonly choose not to exercise it.

The equity of redemption was recognised out of sympathy for the mortgagor, who was often placed in an invidious position by the stronger bargaining power of the mortgagee. He was forced to agree to a mortgage with a very short repayment date or on very harsh terms because he needed money. Equity not only recognised the mortgagor's right to redeem at any time, it also scrutinised other clauses in mortgage agreements to ensure that they were not an implied restriction on the right to redeem or an unconscionable use of bargaining power.

Besides the right to redeem at any time, equity also recognised other rights as being vested in the mortgagor. The sum total of the mortgagor's rights constituted the equity of redemption. This was an equitable interest belonging to the mortgagor which could itself be mortgaged.

I: Creation of a Mortgage/Types of Mortgage

A mortgage involves the transfer of an interest in land as security for a debt. As with all land transfers, the mortgage may be a legal or equitable mortgage; it may involve a transfer of the absolute or the equitable interest in land. It may be a transfer of freehold or leasehold ownership.

Mortgages of freeholds

Legal mortgages

There are two ways in which the legal estate in land can be mortgaged. The first is by the transfer of the freehold ownership in that land, with a proviso for redemption. The second is by the creation of a lease in favour of the mortgagee which, although for a specific number of years, is subject to the proviso that it will end early on discharge of the mortgage. The advantage of the second method is that it allows successive mortgages of the freehold to be created through the mechanism of granting leases of the reversion. The legal estate may also be mortgaged by statutory mortgage under section 26 of the Conveyancing Act 1881, but this method is rarely used.

Equitable mortgages

Once again, there are several types. An equitable mortgage may arise where there is an agreement to create a legal mortgage but where no deed of conveyance has been executed. The correct formalities for the creation of a legal mortgage have not been satisfied. However, equity treats an agreement for a mortgage as being as good as a mortgage. This gives rise to a transfer of the equitable interest to the mortgagee.

Secondly, there may be a mortgage of an equitable interest. The person may mortgage his equity of redemption, if he has already a legal mortgage, or he may mortgage an interest held by him as a beneficiary under a trust.

Thirdly, there may be an equitable mortgage by deposit of title deeds. This does not have to be in writing. The mere deposit of the title deeds constitutes a sufficient act of part performance to satisfy the Statute of Frauds. This form of mortgage is a popular one with Irish banks, but often creates evidentiary problems for them at a later date when the customer alleges that the title deeds were lodged only for safekeeping.

Mortgages of leaseholds

Legal mortgages of leases may be created by assignment, by sub-lease or under the Conveyancing Act 1881. Equitable mortgages of leaseholds may be created in the same ways as equitable mortgages of freeholds.

Mortgages of interests in registered land

Special principles apply as regards the creation of mortgages over registered land. Legal mortgages over registered land can only be created by registered charge. This only becomes effective when it is registered on the Register and the Registrar of Titles gives the chargeholder a certificate of charge. The borrower remains the registered legal owner of the land. A registered charge is normally inferior to a mortgage. However, under the Registration of Title Act 1964, a registered chargeholder has all the powers of sale and receivership possessed by a mortgagee by deed. However, the registered chargeholder has no automatic right to possession.

It is possible to create equitable mortgages of registered land which are not revealed by the Register.

II: EQUITY'S SCRUTINY OF TERMS IN MORTGAGE AGREEMENTS

Terms which unfairly restrict the right to redeem

Certain provisions in mortgages may be struck down because they unfairly restrict the mortgagor's right to redeem:

(a)   Clauses which expressly state that there is no right to redeem. These clauses are always invalid.

(b)   Clauses which confer an option to purchase on the mortgagee. These clauses are automatically void. If the mortgagee were to exercise this option, the mortgagor's right to redeem would be completely ineffective. Such clauses may however be upheld if they can be seen as being part of a different transaction from the mortgage.

(c)   Clauses which postpone the right to redeem. Such clauses are valid, provided that:

(i)   they are not too harsh;

(ii)   they do not take away all value from the equity of redemption by making the right to redeem illusory, e.g. *Fairclough v. Swan Brewery Co. Ltd.* ([1912] A.C. 565).

(d)   Collateral advantages. Collateral advantages are extra rights which are conferred on a mortgagee over and above his right to repayment of the money loaned. The right to claim interest on the loan would not be a collateral advantage since it constitutes an integral part of repayment. However, common examples of collateral advantages are to be seen in the tied-house agreements entered into between breweries and publicans, whereby the brewery lends the publican the money to buy the pub, and the publican covenants, as part of the mortgage agreement, only to sell beer from that particular brewery.

Collateral advantages which persist after redemption are unenforceable since to uphold them would conflict with the equity of redemption, which says that on repayment of the loan and interest the mortgagor ought to regain ownership free from any restraints. This was laid down in the case of *Noakes & Co. Ltd. v. Rice* ([1902] A.C. 24) where a tied-house agreement which purported to persist after re-demption was held unenforceable.

Noakes & Co. Ltd. v. Rice was applied in two subsequent cases; *Browne v. Ryan* ([1901] 2 I.R. 653) and *Bradley v. Carritt* ([1903] A.C. 253). In *Browne v. Ryan* the mortgagor agreed to sell the mortgaged land within 12 months through the mortgagee who was an auction-eer. The clause was designed to generate business for the mortgagee. Even if he redeemed the mortgage before the 12 months were up, he was still obliged to sell his land. For this reason, the clause was struck down as conflicting with the equity of redemption.

In *Bradley v. Carritt* a number of shares in a tea company were mortgaged. One aim of the mortgage was to give the mortgagee, who was a tea broker, the controlling interest in the tea company. The mortgage provided that if the mortgagee did not get the brokerage for the sale of the company's tea, the mortgagor would pay him the amount of the commission that the mortgagee would have got as broker. Once again, this clause was held to be unenforceable because the collateral advantage persisted even after the mortgage was re-deemed.

However, as with options to purchase, collateral advantages which persist after redemption may be permissible provided that they are contained in a separate transaction from the mortgage.

This has always been the case in relation to options to purchase, but was established in relation to collateral advantages by the case of *Kreglinger v. New Patagonia Meat and Cold Storage Co. Ltd.* ([1914] A.C. 25). In that case it was held that a collateral advantage which persisted after redemption was enforceable even though it was granted at the same time and contained in the same document as the mortgage. The House of Lords found nonetheless that the grant of a collateral ad-vantage was a separate transaction from the mortgage.

Terms which are unduly harsh or unconscionable

Equity may strike out clauses in mortgage agreements on the ground that they are too harsh. It has been stated that a clause postponing the right to redeem may be struck down on the grounds of unconscion-ability. Another type of clause vulnerable to an unconscionability find-ing is the collateral advantage.

Originally, equity was very suspicious of collateral advantages. Moneylending legislation provided for a maximum rate of interest on loans. The device of collateral advantages was used to circumvent this and for this reason equity had a tendency to declare collateral advantages void. However, today collateral advantages are enforceable provided that they are not oppressive or unconscionable. In *Biggs v. Hoddinott* a collateral advantage combined with a postponement clause was held to be permissible.

Biggs v. Hoddinott ([1898] 2 Ch. 307)

Facts: This was a tied-house agreement contained in a mortgage of a pub. It was agreed that the mortgage would not be redeemable for five years and so long as the mortgage continued the mortgagor could not sell any beer other than that of the mortgagee brewery.

Held: the agreement was permissible. Since it only postponed redemption for five years, it did not infringe the equity of redemption. In this case it was stated that there was no presumption that a collateral advantage was obtained by pressure, duress or undue influence. The person alleging unconscionability must bear the burden of proving it.

Unconscionability in this context means morally reprehensible dealing. The court takes into account the harshness of the collateral advantages for the mortgagor, the benefit they confer on the mortgagee and the relative bargaining strengths of both parties.

Cityland Property (Holdings) Ltd. v. Dabrah ([1968] Ch. 166)

Facts: A mortgagor had purchased a freehold estate from a landlord. Previously he had only been a lessee. The landlord said that he could leave some of the purchase price unpaid provided that he gave the landlord a mortgage over the property. The mortgage had to be paid back in amounts which were much greater than the amount of the purchase price left unpaid.

Held: Given the parties' unequal bargaining power, the provisions regarding repayment of the mortgage could not be enforced.

It is worth contrasting the decision in *Cityland* with that reached in the following case.

Multiservice Bookbinding Ltd. v. Marden ([1979] Ch. 84)

Facts: The mortgagor borrowed money in order to expand his business. However, at the same time, the mortgagee wanted to use the mortgage as an investment. It was provided that the amount repayable would be calculated by reference to the Swiss franc. However, the Swiss franc increased dramatically in value against the pound, so the mortgagor had a lot more to pay back. The mortgagor argued that this was unconscionable.

Held: The court rejected the mortgagor's argument, and upheld the clause, because he had got independent legal advice at the time of entering into the mortgage.

Restraint of trade/undue influence

These are other grounds on which equity is prepared to strike down mortgages. Details about them are to be found in any contract law text.

III: RIGHTS OF THE MORTGAGOR

As stated above, the mortgagor is the person who transfers his property to a mortgagee in return for a loan. He is the borrower.

The mortgagor has certain rights, in particular the right to redeem the property. He has a legal right to redeem up to the date specified in the mortgage document and has, after that time, an equitable right to redeem.

Equity is vigilant in protecting the mortgagor's equitable right to redeem. It regards him as having a right to get back the property on repayment free from any clogs and fetters. Therefore, collateral advantages which persist after redemption and options to purchase are generally void unless they can be regarded as part of a separate transaction. We have looked at how various clauses in a mortgage may be void if they try to take away the mortgagor's right to redeem. However, clauses postponing the mortgagor's right to redeem are generally permitted.

The right to redeem may be lost if the mortgagee gets a sale order or a foreclosure order from the court, or if the mortgagee exercises his statutory power of sale (see below).

Normally the mortgagor must give reasonable notice of his intention to redeem or, alternatively, pay six months' interest. The purpose of this requirement is to give the mortgagee the opportunity to look elsewhere to find a replacement investment for his capital. The mortgagor must repay the principal sum, interest and the costs of the mortgagee. The mortgagee is entitled to all reasonable costs.

The mortgagor normally has a *de facto* right to possession after the mortgage has been entered into. Even though the mortgagee may have the technical right to possession, he will not usually exercise this right so as to evict the mortgagor (see below). The mortgagor can still maintain actions to protect his property against third parties. He can bring an action to recover the land against anyone other than the mortgagee or a person claiming through him.

The mortgagor is usually allowed to retain possession of the title deeds but may be required to deliver them up to the mortgagee on request.

The mortgagor may make an *inter vivos* transfer of his equity of redemption to another party, but this party will usually take subject to the mortgage. He cannot sell the property free from the mortgage unless he redeems or gets the mortgagee to join in the conveyance.

IV: RIGHTS OF THE MORTGAGEE

The right to possession

A legal mortgagee is entitled to possession as soon as the ink is dry on the mortgage. This has been established since the case of *Fourmaids Ltd. v. Dudley Marshall (Properties) Ltd.* ([1957] Ch. 317). However, it is uncertain whether equitable mortgagees are entitled to automatic possession. Nonetheless, equitable mortgagees can apply to court for an order granting them possession.

As we have seen, mortgages of registered land are effected by way of registered charge. The holder of a registered charge does not have an automatic right to possession and has to apply to the court.

The right to possession may also be excluded by an express or an implied clause in the mortgage.

Although the right to possession commonly exists, it is very rarely exercised. Mortgagees are reluctant to enter into possession, because, if they do, they have a liability to account for the income produced by the land. They may be held liable to pay compensation to the mortgagor for failure to get the maximum value out of the land. For this reason mortgagees prefer to exercise their power of sale or their power to appoint a receiver.

If they go into possession they may only use the profits from the land to pay off the mortgage debt and interest. In addition they may be penalised if they are not using the land to its maximum financial profit level.

However, in certain circumstances the benefits secured by the mortgagee in gaining possession may outweigh the drawbacks. One example is where the mortgagee is planning to sell the property. He may take possession in anticipation of the sale, since it is easier to sell property with vacant possession than with a sitting mortgagor. If he is an equitable mortgagee or a registered chargee, he may apply for a court order for possession in anticipation of a sale out of court.

The appointment of a receiver

If the mortgagee feels that the mortgaged property is not being adequately managed by the mortgagor, but he has no wish to sell it, he may decide to exercise his right to appoint a receiver to manage the property. This right may be expressly granted by the mortgage agreement, but assuming that it is not, the mortgagee has a statutory power to appoint a receiver under section 19(1)(iii) of the Conveyancing Act 1881. This provision applies to all mortgages created by deed but may be excluded by a provision to the contrary in the mortgage. If the mortgage has not been created by deed, then the mortgagee can apply to the court to have a receiver appointed under the Supreme Court of Judicature (Ireland) Act 1877. The court will grant this application where it is just and convenient to do so.

The right under section 19(1)(iii) does not arise until the preconditions for the statutory power of sale are satisfied, *i.e.* the mortgage money must be overdue, and in addition the mortgagee must have become entitled to exercise the statutory power of sale under section 20 of the 1881 Act (see below).

The mortgagor has a discretion as to whom he appoints as receiver. The appointment must be in writing. The receiver is the agent of the mortgagee and the mortgagee is liable for his defaults unless the mortgage deed provides otherwise. However, by appointing a receiver the mortgagee cannot be regarded as taking possession and so is not strictly liable to account.

The power of sale

There may be an express clause in the mortgage giving the mortgagee the power of sale. Even if this is not present, there is a statutory power of sale under section 19(1)(i) of the Conveyancing Act 1881. This provision applies to all mortgages created by deed unless excluded by a contrary provision in the mortgage agreement. If the mortgage is not created by deed then it is necessary to apply to the court for a court order for sale. This procedure is detailed later.

The statutory power of sale comes into play whenever:

(a)   the mortgage payments are overdue;

(b)   one of three further conditions laid down in section 20 is
        satisfied.

There is a distinction between the power of sale arising and becom-
ing exercisable. Once (a) is satisfied, the power of sale arises. However, the power only becomes exercisable when (b) is present.

The conditions laid down in section 20 are as follows:

(i)   A notice must have been served on the mortgagor requir-
        ing payment of the overdue money, followed by a failure
        on the part of the mortgagor to make payment within three
        months of the service of the notice.

(ii)   Interest under the mortgage must have been in arrears for
        two months.

(iii)   A covenant in the mortgage deed (other than a repayment
        covenant) must have been breached.

Only one of these conditions has to be satisfied in order for the power
of sale to become exercisable.

When the statutory or contractual power of sale arises, it is up to
the mortgagee to proceed with selling the property. He may decide
how the sale is conducted. However, the mortgagee has a duty to
obtain the best price possible for the property. He must take reasonable care in this regard.

The case of *Holohan v. Friends Provident and Century Life Office* ([1966]
I.R. 1) is a good illustration of this duty. Here, the mortgagees exercised their power of sale over a property without bothering to secure
vacant possession prior to the sale. A property sold without vacant
possession is almost certain to obtain a lower price than one with
vacant possession. The Supreme Court held that there had been a
breach of duty. The pertinent question was: what would the reasonable man, aiming to get the best price available in the circumstances,
do in this situation? In the particular situation in hand, the reasonable
man would have postponed the sale until vacant possession could be
achieved.

Extremely close scrutiny of sales by a mortgagee takes place when
the mortgagee presumes to sell to a company in which he is a share-
holder. He is not prohibited from selling to such a company, but he
must show that his decision was in accordance with expert advice.

In addition the mortgagee must distribute the purchase money
properly. The proceeds of sale must be applied by the mortgagee in

discharge of incumbrances such as prior mortgages. Then any costs of the sale should be disbursed. The purchase monies are then used to pay the mortgage debt and interest. The balance is then paid to the mortgagor.

The purchaser who buys from a mortgagee who has acted outside the terms of section 19(1)(i) is protected provided that the mortgage debt was due at the time of the sale. Once this is shown, it is not necessary for a prospective purchaser to enquire as to whether one of the three conditions listed above has been satisfied.

As stated above, when a mortgagee has no contractual or statutory power of sale he may apply for a court order for sale of the property. The court will make a well-charging order stating that the mortgage is valid. This will be followed by an order for sale. The court will usually place a stay on the order for sale. The reason for this is to give the mortgagor the chance to discharge the debt. A court sale proceeds by way of auction. The court appoints the auctioneer, determines the reserve price and the purchase money is paid into court. However, the person who obtained the order for sale is still regarded as the vendor.

Foreclosure

This is the most drastic remedy available to the mortgagee. Basically, a court order of foreclosure extinguishes the mortgagor's equity of redemption by declaring the mortgagee the absolute owner of the property. This may result in substantial profit for the mortgagee.

Foreclosure affects both the mortgagor and any subsequent mortgagees detrimentally. Hence, they must all be made parties to the action.

Because foreclosure is such a harsh remedy, Irish courts are very reluctant to grant it. In *Bruce v. Brophy* ([1906] 1 I.R. 611) it was described as a remedy which would only be ordered in special circumstances. The court declined to comment as to when these circumstances might arise.

V: Judgment Mortgages

When one person is found by the court to owe money to another, the court may grant the creditor a judgment mortgage over the debtor's land. The creditor has the right to have the land sold and the proceeds used to discharge his debt.

However, any creditor who wishes to obtain a judgment mortgage must follow the procedure laid down by the Judgment Mortgage (Ireland) Acts 1850–58. He must file an affidavit in the court where the judgment was granted. The affidavit must contain details of the court, the title of the action and the date and amount of the judgment awarded against the defendant. The relevant parties and the land over which the mortgage is sought must be identified.

The filing of the affidavit transfers all of the land in question to the creditor and vests it in him subject to the debtor's right to redeem on paying the outstanding money. Thus, the creditor is given the status of a mortgagee.

The creditor now has a judgment mortgage and he may enforce his rights under the mortgage by seeking a well-charging order and an order for the sale of the land.

Chapter 14

Succession Law

Succession law deals with what happens to an individual's property when he or she dies. It regulates the transfer of a person's real and personal property on death. To the extent that succession law deals with the transfer of personal property on death, it goes beyond the strict confines of a land law course, which would deal with the law of real property only. However, the rules for transfer of real and personal property on death are similar, and are commonly taught together as part of a land law course. So this is how they will be dealt with here.

There are two different sets of rules for distributing an individual's property on his or her death. Which set of rules is applied depends on whether the individual has made a will or not. A will is a document made by the deceased directing the distribution of his property in a particular way after his death. If an individual has made a valid will, he dies testate. His property is divided according to the terms of his will, with some potential statutory modifications.

For example, if an individual leaves his property away from his family in his will, so as to leave his wife destitute and his children poverty-stricken, this can be remedied by the wife and children invoking the rights conferred on them by Part IX of the Succession Act 1965. To this extent, statutory provisions may override the terms of a will.

On an entirely different issue, if an individual dies without having made a valid will, he dies intestate. His property is divided according to the rules on intestate succession. These rules are laid down in the Succession Act.

I: WILLS

A will is a disposition executed by an individual prior to his death in which he outlines the way in which he would like his property to be distributed on his death. The person making the will is known as the testator if he is a man and the testatrix if a woman.

There is obviously a risk of forged wills, and so certain formal requirements have been introduced to prevent this. The current set of formalities are contained in the Succession Act 1965. If a will does not satisfy these it cannot be enforced and the result is that the deceased dies intestate (without a valid will) and the rules on intestacy have to be applied.

Requirements for a valid will

(a) Capacity

Basically, what this means is that the testator (the person making the will) must be of sound mind and of age (over the age of 18, or married).

There have been two recent cases where wills were challenged on the ground that the testator was not of sound disposing mind at the time the will was made. In *Blackall v. Blackall* (unreported, Supreme Court, April 1, 1998) and *O'Donnell v. O'Donnell* (unreported, High Court, Kelly J., March 24, 1999) both challenges were rejected. Kelly J. in the latter case quoted from the High Court judgment of McCracken J. in *Blackall* (unreported, June 28, 1996) which had been affirmed by the Supreme Court.

McCracken J. stated as follows:

"The onus of proving the formal validity of a will is undoubtedly on the person who propounds the will, but where there is a challenge to a will based on the state of knowledge or state of health of the testator, the onus is on the person who challenges the will."

The testator in *O'Donnell* had been a paranoid schizophrenic for many years. However, Kelly J. accepted medical evidence to the effect that his condition was both controllable and controlled by medication. The fact that the deceased was eccentric in some respects did not mean that he was incapable of making a will. Remarks that the deceased made to his solicitor at the time of signing the will "displayed considerable insight" and were "absolutely accurate". The will itself was "rational, clear, insightful and sensible". The presumption of sound disposing mind had not been rebutted.

(b) Formal requirements

(i)   Writing. The Succession Act 1965 mirrors previous legislation by requiring that a will be in writing, signed at the bottom by the testator, and that his signature be witnessed by two or more witnesses who themselves sign the will to verify that they have witnessed the testator's signature or his acknowledgment of same.

N.B. A will made by tape recorder, or video tape, is not valid because it is not in writing, even though it is recorded on a permanent record.

(ii) The will must be signed by the testator, or by someone directed by him.

Placing of the signature. The signature must be at the foot of the will. Any substantive provisions which follow the signature will make it invalid. However, the Act provides that a space may intervene between the foot of the will or the signature, and that the signature may be on a separate page at the end of the will.

The signature itself:

- The signature does not have to be legible. This was established by *In b. Kieran* ([1933] I.R. 22).
- Any mark made by the testator intended by him as his signature can qualify as his signature. This is important for illiterate testators. In the case of *Re Glynn* ([1990] 2 I.R. 326) an "X" was held sufficient.
- However, the imprint of a seal is not enough.
- Sometimes the testator may not sign his real name but may use a nickname or family name by which he is generally known, *e.g.* "Your Loving Mother", as occurred in *In b. Cook* ([1960] 1 W.L.R. 353). This too is permissible.
- The Act provides that the testator may direct someone else to sign the will on his behalf, *e.g.* if he is too weak to sign. It has been stated in *In b. McLoughlin* ([1936] I.R. 223) that it is acceptable for the person so directed to sign not in the testator's name but in his own name. If the person directed signs the testator's name, it is uncertain whether the will is invalid or not. The direction to the signing person by the testator must be made in the presence of witnesses.
- Sometimes the testator has to be aided to write his signature by someone else, *e.g.* a nurse's help is needed to aid him in moving the pen. In *Fulton v. Kee* ([1961] N.I. 1) it was held that the assisted mark counts as the signature of the testator provided that he made an independent physical contribution to the making of the mark. Even if he did not make an independent

physical contribution it is arguable that the signature was valid on the grounds that he impliedly directed the nurse to sign for him in the event that he was unable to do so.

The judicial interpretation of the signature requirement has been quite flexible. The reason for this is that a further rule exists to safeguard the testator. The witnessing requirements require that the testator either make or acknowledge the signature as his in the presence of two witnesses. So an illegible mark may constitute a signature, but it will not ground a valid will unless made in front of witnesses.

(iii)   The will must be witnessed. There must be two or more witnesses. The signature must be either made or acknowledged in their presence. Then the witnesses must sign the will to say that they have witnessed this. Again, initials or a mark will suffice as the witness's signature.

• The witnesses do not have to, and usually do not, see the contents of the will. What happens is that the substantive part of the will is covered over with a page, with only the signature at the bottom showing. The testator either makes this signature in the presence of the witnesses, or acknowledges it as his own in their presence. Then they sign to say that they have witnessed the signature. The witness's signature does not have to be under the testator's signature and can be on any part of the will.

• The witness must actually see the signing or acknowledgment of the signature. A blind person cannot be a valid witness. Similarly, a witness whose path of vision is obscured at the crucial moment of signature or acknowledgment cannot be a valid witness.

• The witness requirements are a crucial part of the formality requirements, particularly given the fact that the signature requirements are so flexible. For this reason it is important that a witness's signature be genuine and not be influenced by any considerations of personal gain. Therefore a witness cannot receive any gift under a will they have witnessed. Any gifts to witnesses or to the spouses of witnesses are void. It is important to note that the chosen solution in this case is not to make the will invalid, but to render the gifts to the witnesses void.

This rule is illustrated by the case of *Re Bravda* ([1968] 1 W.L.R. 479). A father executed a will leaving his property between his two daughters. There were four witnesses to the will, two of whom unfortunately were the daughters. For this reason the gifts to the daughters were invalid. It did not matter that they were superfluous witnesses.

- However, if the gift to the witness is a gift to him as trustee, or if the gift is on its face to someone else but the witness takes as beneficiary under a secret trust (a trust *dehors* the will), the gift is valid.

Additions and changes to a will

It is a core principle of the Succession Act that anything which comes after the signature is void. This includes provisions which come after the signature in time, as well as those provisions which come after it in the document itself. Therefore any crossings out on the will which take place subject to the testator's signature are void. There is a presumption that any alterations to the body of the will have taken place after signature and therefore are invalid. This presumption may be rebutted.

If a testator wants to make alterations to his will he may do this in one of three ways:

1. He may revoke the original will and execute an entirely new one.
2. He may execute a codicil or supplementary provision to the will containing the alterations. To be valid, this codicil must be signed and witnessed in the same way as the original will.
3. He may write the alterations in on the original will. However, each individual alteration must be signed and witnessed.

Revoking a will

Express revocation may be achieved either by executing a formal document which states that it is revoking the will, or by some act of revocation, *e.g.* destruction of the will with the intention to revoke. N.B. Mere destruction of the will *per se* will not constitute a revocation unless such destruction is coupled with an intention on the part of the testator to revoke.

A will is automatically revoked on marriage and may be revoked if a completely new will is made, the terms of which are inconsistent with that of the previous will.

Once a will is revoked, it can never be revived. The only way around the problem is to execute a new will.

Administration of a will

Assume the existence of a valid will, not revoked at any time before the testator's death. We now have to consider how the estate of someone who dies testate is administered on their death.

On the death of a testator, his property automatically vests in the persons named as executors in the will, to be distributed by them to the beneficiaries named in the will. The executors have to apply for a grant of representation before they can administer the property. This process of applying for a grant of representation is also known as proving the will, admitting the will to probate, or getting a grant of probate.

If a will has been lost, its contents may be reconstructed by the court, provided that it has not been revoked by destruction.

Representation will only be granted by the court/probate office if they are satisfied that there is a valid will.

If there is nobody named as executor under the will, or the person named as executor declines his duties, or the deceased dies intestate, then the property of the deceased vests in the Master of the High Court until such time as administrators are appointed. The beneficiaries under the will or on intestacy should apply to the court for a grant of representation to ask the court to appoint administrators. This is known as applying for letters of administration. Once letters of administration have been granted, the newly appointed administrators have the same rights and duties as executors who have been given a grant of representation. Both executors and administrators may be described as the deceased's personal representatives and they shall be referred to together under this title hereafter.

Once a grant of representation/letters of administration has been made, the deceased's property devolves to the personal representatives and the process of dealing with his estate begins. Personal representatives will get custody of all the documents of title and will pay off all debts. The 1965 Act lays down the order in which certain debts or liabilities should be paid off.

After paying off the debts of the deceased, the question of distributing his property to the beneficiaries under his will or on intestacy arises. The personal representative has a general obligation to distribute the estate as soon as possible after the deceased's death. As stated already, the property of a deceased person vests on the personal representatives on death or when letters of administration are granted, and they are stated to hold the estate as trustees for the persons who are entitled to it. This does not mean that the beneficiaries under the will or intestacy have a beneficial interest in the property while it is in the hands of the personal representatives. The personal representatives own the property absolutely, and are merely subject to a fiduciary obligation in respect thereof.

Personal representatives are entitled to sell any assets of the estate for the purposes of paying debts or distributing the estate among persons who are entitled to it. But if someone is specifically entitled to the asset under the will the personal representatives must, so far as practicable, give effect to such an individual's wishes. They also have a right of appropriation. Under section 55 they may apply a specific item of property in its existing form towards the satisfaction of a person's share in the estate. However, an appropriation of this nature cannot affect any specific devise or bequest. The court may, at its discretion, prohibit the appropriation on the application of any one of the persons entitled under the will.

Often the personal representatives will have difficulty ascertaining from the terms of a will which individuals are meant to benefit. The following principles are helpful.

Interpretation of wills

A will speaks from death
When interpreting a will, one does not look at the situation at the time the will was made, but rather at the situation at the time the testator died. Therefore property which was acquired by the testator after he made the will may still be distributed under the will. In addition, gifts to people who predeceased the testator are invalid and fall into the residue, if there is a residue clause, or otherwise fall to be distributed on intestacy (a partial intestacy). This is known as the doctrine of lapse.

There is one exception to the doctrine of lapse: if a parent makes a gift to their child, who dies before them, and that child has issue living at the time of the grandparent's death, the gift does not lapse (section 98 of the Succession Act). This principle was applied in *Moorehead v. Tiilikainen* ([1999] 2 I.L.R.M. 471) where a daughter predeceased her mother. However, the result in this case probably conflicted with the policy of section 98 to some extent. The daughter died intestate and her husband received two-thirds of the gift made to her by her mother. The three grandchildren merely received one-ninth of the gift each.

The armchair principle

When the court is interpreting a will it must put itself in the same position as the testator, see the world through his eyes, and be aware of the phrases he used in his lifetime to describe things. This is known as the armchair principle, the judge must sit in the testator's chair, and get within his mindset.

An example of the application of the armchair principle can be found in *Thorn v. Dickens* ([1906] W.N. 54). Here a testator left all his property to "mother". Evidence was admitted that he had been in the habit of using the term "mother" to refer to his wife.

The armchair principle primarily relates to the testator's use of language. If there is evidence that the testator was in the habit of using a particular word to refer to a particular person or thing during his lifetime, and he has used this word in his will, evidence can be admitted that he used this word to refer to a particular person or thing. So the scope for admission of evidence under the armchair principle is quite limited. The limits of the armchair principle were shown in *Re Julian* ([1950] I.R. 57).

Re Julian involved an interpretation of the will of an old lady who had left her money to the Seamen's Institute, Sir John Rogerson's Quay, Dublin. The testatrix was a Protestant and the only Seamen's Institute at Sir John Rogerson's Quay was the Catholic Seamen's Institute. There was a Protestant Seamen's Institute located on Eden Quay. Evidence was sought to be admitted that when the old lady was drawing up her will she asked her lawyer for the address of the Protestant Seamen's Institute. He looked up the directory, and saw only one institute listed, the Seamen's Institute, Sir John Rogerson's Quay. So he put this title and address down.

However, it was held that evidence of the circumstances surrounding the making of the will was not admissible. First of all, the armchair principle was ineffective in the circumstances of the case.

There was an alternative broader principle in the law that extrinsic evidence of circumstances surrounding the making of the will generally could be admitted in cases of ambiguity. The trial judge in *Re Julian* (and this is a much argued point) appeared to say that there was an ambiguity on the facts, but that the common law principle only allowed extrinsic evidence in respect of a particular type of ambiguity, and that the ambiguity in *Re Julian* was not of this type. It was not a description which applied equally to two things, but one which applied partly to one thing and partly to another, but wholly accurately to neither. Extrinsic evidence was not admissible to resolve the latter kind of ambiguity.

Extrinsic evidence and section 90 of the Succession Act 1965
Subsequent to *Re Julian* the 1965 Succession Act was enacted and section 90 provided as follows:

> "Extrinsic evidence shall be admissible to show the intention
> of the testator and to assist in the construction of, or to
> explain any contradiction in, a will."

Did this provision change the law in *Re Julian*? The issue has been discussed by Irish courts in a number of post-1965 cases.

First, in *Rowe v. Law* ([1978] I.R. 55) the Supreme Court was called upon to decide whether extrinsic evidence could be admitted to change the contents of a will even where there was no ambiguity on the face of the will. The answer of the majority of the Supreme Court was in the negative. O'Higgins C.J. delivered a strong dissent.

The three arguments voiced by the majority in support of their conclusion were as follows:

(i)   An interpretation of the wording of section 90 indicated that extrinsic evidence was only admissible in cases of ambiguity. With respect, this argument was incorrect.

(ii)   Section 90 should be interpreted in the context of the Succession Act as a whole.

(iii)   Policy considerations.

Arguments (ii) and (iii) were the more compelling. Henchy J. feared that allowing widespread extrinsic evidence of intention would be "a sweeping and disruptive change, fraught with possibilities for mistake and uncertainty". Griffin J. pointed out further dangers. Section 90 provided no controls on the admission of extrinsic evidence. Its terms did not restrict the admission of extrinsic evidence to documents made around the time of the making of the will. On the terms of section 90, evidence from years before or years after could be admitted. Section 90 should be controlled as much as possible.

In his dissent, O'Higgins C.J. said that section 90 was clearly intended to enact a change in the law, and must be interpreted in this way. He felt that *Re Julian* would be decided the same way under the majority's interpretation of section 90; this destroyed any justification for enacting this section. He also based his conclusion on the wording of section 90.

Subsequent cases were *Lindsay v. Tomlinson* (unreported, High Court, February 13, 1996) where there was a bequest to the National Society for the Prevention of Cruelty to Animals (Dogs and Cats Home), 1 Grand Canal quay. This description did not fully apply to any existing body. There were two bodies to whom it partially applied: the Dublin Society for the Prevention of Cruelty to Animals and the Irish Society for the Prevention of Cruelty to Animals. It was held that there was an ambiguity here and evidence could be given of the testator's relationship with the first institution throughout the last few years of her life in order to show that she intended to leave it to them.

However, in *Re Julian* which was a very similar case extrinsic evidence was not admissible. The judge in the case specifically said that the extrinsic evidence was being excluded not because there was no ambiguity but because the ambiguity was not of the right type. To this extent, *Re Julian* could be decided otherwise today and section 90 did change it.

This was recognised by Keane J. in his very clear judgment in *Re Collins: O'Connell v. Bank of Ireland* ([1998] 2 I.R. 596). Here an attempt was made to get the Supreme Court to overrule *Rowe v. Law*, relying on O'Higgins C.J.'s minority reasoning in this case. However, as Keane J. pointed out, some of this reasoning was flawed. Section 90 was intended to effect, and did effect, a change in the law. In particular he rejected O'Higgins C.J.'s view that section 90 would have made no difference to the result in *Re Julian*. *Rowe v. Law* was unequivocally affirmed, and the Supreme Court decision in *Re Curtin Deceased* ([1991] 2 I.R. 562) which some commentators had thought marked a departure from *Rowe*, was distinguished as an example of the application of the principle that a will should be construed in order to prevent an intestacy.

The position now is that extrinsic evidence may only be admitted if there is an ambiguity on the face of the will, for the purpose of resolving that ambiguity. In *Lynch v. Burke* (unreported, High Court, McCracken J., July 30, 1999) the will was open to two different constructions. Extrinsic evidence was therefore admitted under section 90.

However, on examination of the extrinsic evidence the judge found himself unable to take it into account in interpreting the will. The particular extrinsic evidence in hand did not support either of the alternative constructions. The language of the will would have to be severely stretched to give effect to the intention evidenced in the extrinsic evidence. It was felt that extrinsic evidence should only be used in interpreting a will if to do so would resolve an ambiguity. Here the extrinsic evidence did not resolve anything; it merely raised more problems and therefore it should be discounted.

Lynch v. Burke illustrates the point that even if extrinsic evidence is admitted under section 90, and clearly shows the intention of the testator, it may on some occasions be impossible to interpret the will so as to give effect to that intention. Even when extrinsic evidence is admitted, it cannot be used so as to do violence to the language of the will.

II: STATUTORY RIGHTS OF SPOUSES AND CHILDREN UNDER THE SUCCESSION ACT

For centuries the principle of freedom of testation was inherent in the law. Then the Succession Act 1965 introduced certain provisions to protect the family of a deceased. It gave both a spouse and a child of the deceased the right to override the terms of his will and to claim a share in the deceased's property to which they were not entitled under the will.

In addition, it provided that a testator could not circumvent the terms of the Succession Act by disposing of his property to others prior to his death. Section 121 applies to gifts of the testator's estate within the three years preceding his death. If the court finds that the disposition was made for the purpose of defeating or substantially diminishing the share of the testator's spouse or the children, the court may order that the disposition may be deemed to be a bequest by will which forms part of the deceased's estate.

Spousal rights under section 111

(a) The spouse of a deceased has a right to one-half of the deceased's estate if there are no children and a one-third if there are children
If the spouse has been left nothing under the will, she automatically gets her legal right share.

If the spouse has been left a gift under the will, she can choose either this or her legal right share. Usually the spouse will choose whichever is larger in value. If the gift left to her under the will is lesser in value but has sentimental associations, she can take it in part satisfaction of her legal right share. The Succession Act states that a spouse may elect to take any bequest given to her under the will in part satisfaction of her legal right share.

However, when there is a gift under the will it is necessary for the spouse to inform the personal representatives that she wishes to take the legal right share instead of the gift under the will. She must positively elect in favour of the legal right share. If she fails to so inform them she will only get the gift under the will. For this reason it is very important that the personal representatives notify the spouse in writing of her right to elect for the legal right share.

This duty of positive election only arises where there is a gift to the spouse under the will. If the spouse gets nothing under the will, the legal right share vests automatically. There is no need for an election. This point was demonstrated by *O'Dwyer v. Keegan* ([1997] 2 I.L.R.M. 401). In this case a testator died 12 hours before his wife, to whom he had left nothing in his will. The question was whether the wife's heirs could claim her legal right share. The issue was whether the legal right share passed to her automatically on her husband's death, despite the fact that she was comatose at the time. The Supreme Court upheld the claim of the wife's heirs. She had obtained the legal right share automatically on her husband's death. The position would have been different had the husband left the wife a gift under the will.

It must also be noted that if a gift under a will is specifically expressed to be in addition to the spouse's legal right share, the spouse will get both the gift under the will and the legal right share.

(b) The right to compel the personal representatives to appropriate the dwelling-house

As well as her right to the legal right share, the surviving spouse also has a right to compel the personal representatives to appropriate a dwelling-house in which she was living at the time of the deceased's death, and its contents, in satisfaction of her legal right share and/or the share of a dependent child under the will or section 117. Once again, the personal representatives have a duty to inform her of this right.

This right of appropriation should not be confused with the general right that the personal representatives may have to appropriate any part of the estate on the application of any beneficiary in satisfaction of their share.

Children's rights under section 117

Unlike the spouse's legal right share, this right is not automatic, but depends on the discretion of the court. The provision itself is vague, and its operation has to be demonstrated by reference to case law.

Section 117 of the Succession Act provides that where the court is of the opinion that the testator has failed in his moral duty to make proper provision for the child in accordance with his means, the court may order that just provision be made for the child out of the estate.

Child includes adopted and illegitimate children, and also children who are of age. The obligation under section 117 is not confined to minors, nor to children of the deceased who were financially dependent on him.

An application under section 117 must be made within six months from the first taking out of representation of the deceased's estate.

Whether a section 117 order will be granted depends on the following considerations laid down by Kenny J. in *Re G.M.* ((1972) 106 I.L.T.R. 82). These guidelines were approved by the Supreme Court in *C.C. v. W.C* ([1990] 2 I.R. 143). The courts had to pay particular attention to the following factors:

- The number of the testator's children, their ages and positions in life.
- The means of the testator.
- The age of the applicant child.
- The children's financial position and prospects in life.
- Whether the testator had made financial provision for the applicant child during his life.

Taking into account the above factors, the testator must ask what a prudent and just parent would have done in this position. The standard is not that of the average parent, but of the prudent and just parent.

Two recent cases on section 117 merit discussion. In *Re L.B.; E.B. v. S.S.* ([1998] 2 I.L.R.M. 141) the plaintiff, aged forty, instituted proceedings under section 117, claiming that his mother had failed in her moral duty to provide for him. His mother, who had died possessed of a considerable estate, had left most of her estate to charity. The plaintiff had had problems with drugs in the past, was separated from his wife, was unemployed and an alcoholic at the time of his mother's death. It was held that there had been no failure of moral duty on the part of the mother. The plaintiff's father, from whom the mother had inherited her property, had paid for him to go back to university when the plaintiff was in his late twenties. In addition, the plaintiff's father had provided him with a house in which he had lived with his family.

Keane J. stated that in deciding the extent of the mother's moral duty the circumstances at the time of her death were to be looked at. It was irrelevant that the plaintiff had subsequently beaten his addictions. In this case there was no failure of duty. The testatrix may have thought that the provision of money to her son in the past had had bad results. It was also stated that failure to provide for grandchildren can never be in breach of section 117 which only refers to a moral duty to children.

In *McDonald v. Norris* ([2000] 1 I.L.R.M. 382) the section 117 applicant had had an acrimonious relationship with his father. He had been taken out of school aged 14 to work on the family farm when his father had been injured in an accident. He did all the work on the farm, his father receiving the profits except for the earnings from some acres of tillage and a quarry. The son received no wages. The father went to live with his sister-in-law's family and grew distant from the son after the son's marriage. He then tried to throw the son off the farm. The son refused to obey a court order to leave the farm and spent 12 months in prison for contempt. While he was in prison the father gave some of the farm to his other son and sold yet another part. There was bad feeling against the father in the neighbourhood for his behaviour and the son did nothing to stop it. The father left all his property to his sister-in-law's child.

It was held that the son was entitled to what was left of the farm. The father had deprived his son of an education and a chance of an independent career. He had received the son's unpaid labour on the farm for many years. It was accepted that the son had to some extent failed in his moral duty towards his parent, and that his share under section 117 would reduce accordingly but the father's failure had been much greater. He had already financially provided for his in-laws during his life, so he could not be said to have been under a moral obligation to them at the time of his death. It was recognised that moral duties to third parties might be taken into account in reducing a child's share, although this had not been specifically stated in the section.

Barron J.'s Supreme Court judgment contrasts sharply with the

High Court judgment of McCracken J. in the case (reported at [1999] 1 I.L.R.M. 270). The two judges had differing views on who was most to blame for the unfortunate incidents which had occurred. They also had different opinions on whether the benefits which the son had received from the farm should be taken into account in assessing his share. It was stated by the Supreme Court that the kind of benefits, receipt of which would justify reducing a child's share under section 117, should relate to the funding of education, the provision of money or the transfer of property. The benefits received by the son were not of this nature.

III: INTESTACY

There are two forms of intestacy: total intestacy and partial intestacy. Total intestacy occurs where someone dies without having made a valid will. Partial intestacy occurs where someone has made a valid will, but it do not cover all the testator's property.

Total intestacy: distribution of estate

Deciding how property should be distributed on intestacy is a two-stage process.

Stage 1

The first stage involves asking a series of questions, in descending order. If one of those questions is answered affirmatively, there is no need to go on to the next question.

- First, does the deceased have a spouse and/or descendants living? If so, distribution according to Class 1 rules.
- If not, does the deceased have parents living? If so, distribution according to Class 2 rules.
- If not, does the deceased have brothers and sisters, or children of brothers and sisters, living? If so, distribution according to Class 3 rules.
- If not, does the deceased have any next-of-kin (descendants from a common ancestor) living? If yes, distribution according to Class 4 rules. If no, distribution according to Class 5 rules the property goes to the State as ultimate intestate successor.

Stage 2

After it has been decided which of the above classes of rules are applicable, those rules are then applied.

Class 1 rules

These apply when there is a spouse and/or issue living. If there is both a spouse and issue, the spouse gets two-thirds of the estate and the issue get one-third. The term "issue" includes all blood descendants and the method of distribution as between the issue is usually *per stirpes*. In other words, grandchildren of the deceased only take if their parent is dead, and the cumulative share of the children of a deceased descendant cannot exceed the share which their parent would have been received had they been alive.

If there is a spouse, but no issue, the spouse gets the whole estate. If there is issue, but no spouse, the issue get the whole estate with distribution *per stirpes*.

Class 2 rules

These apply if there is no spouse or issue of the deceased, but one or both of his parents are alive. In that case, the surviving parent(s) get the whole estate. If both parents are alive, the estate is divided equally between them. If only one parent is alive, they get the whole estate.

Class 3 rules

If there is no spouse, issue or parents then this set of rules is applied. If all the siblings of the deceased are alive, they take equally. If one or more of the siblings are deceased then their share is divided among their children. If all the siblings are deceased, then their children take per capita. However, grandchildren of the siblings cannot take anything under this set of rules, even if their parents and grandparents are both dead. This is not *per stirpes* distribution, although it may at first glance resemble it.

Class 4 rules

If there is no spouse, issue, parents or siblings/children of siblings then this set of rules applies. Are there next-of-kin?

Next-of-kin means descendants from a common ancestor, of the nearest degree available. The rules for ascertaining degrees of relationship are set out in section 71(2) of the 1965 Act.

Briefly summarised, grandparents are the closest next-of-kin. So, if any grandparents of the intestate are alive, they will take the property. If no grandparents are alive, the property is divided equally between the intestate's aunts and uncles. In the unlikely eventuality that there are no grandparents, aunts or uncles alive, but there is a great-grandparent alive, the great-grandparent will get the estate.

If there are no grandparents, great-grandparents, aunts or uncles, then the estate will be divided equally between such grand-aunts and uncles, first cousins and grand-nephews and uncles of the intestate as are alive. If none of the above are alive, then we must move on to first cousins once removed, second cousins and so on.

When applying the next-of-kin rules, it is therefore necessary to ask:

- Are there grandparents of the intestate alive? If not, ask;
- Are there aunts and/or uncles of the intestate alive? If not, ask;
- Are there great-grandparents of the intestate alive? If not, ask;
- Are there grand-nephews and nieces, grand-aunts or uncles, or first cousins of the intestate alive?

For the purposes of all the intestacy rules relatives of the half blood are treated in the same way as relatives of the full blood, and illegitimate children are treated in the same way as legitimate children. The Succession Act specifically provides that adopted children are to be treated as the same as natural children for the purposes of intestacy. If there are no next-of-kin available, the State takes as ultimate intestate successor.

Total intestacy: administration of estate

Obviously the deceased will not have nominated anybody to act as executor, since there was no will. However, anybody who stands to benefit on intestacy may apply to the court to be granted letters of administration. Once the court has appointed administrators, they can apply for a grant of probate. Once this is granted, the property vests in them. Prior to that it had been vested in the Master of the High Court. The administrator gathers in the assets and pays off the debts. As with executors under a will, an administrator on intestacy has the power to sell off part of the estate in order to pay debts, and also the power to appropriate part of the estate for a specific beneficiary. He must then distribute the estate to the persons entitled on intestacy. He must do this by making an assent.

It may be noted that an intestate's spouse has no legal right share on a total intestacy. It is not necessary to give her this right because under the rules on intestacy she is entitled to the whole estate if there are no issue, or two-thirds if there are issue. This is significantly greater than her legal right share.

She still has the right to compel appropriation of the dwelling-house in satisfaction of her share on intestacy, however.

Similarly, a child's right to make section 117 application only applies when the deceased dies wholly or partially testate. It does not apply on a total intestacy.

Partial intestacy

This is a more complicated process than full intestacy. To recap, full intestacy occurs where the deceased has never made a will at all. Partial intestacy occurs when a will has been made, but it does not account for all the deceased's property, and there is no residue clause.

In this case some of the deceased's property falls to be distributed under the will by the executors, while some of it falls to be distributed on intestacy by administrators. A grant of administration will have to be applied for in respect of such of the deceased's property as is not covered by the will.

However, complications ensue in relation to the spousal right under section 111 and the child's right under section 117. These apply in the case of a partial intestacy. If the deceased died partially intestate, the wife and child have a choice between their section 111 and section 117 shares on the one hand, and their gifts under the will and on intestacy combined on the other. In this case, it may often be more profitable for them to reject their statutory shares, *i.e.* for the wife not to exercise her legal right and for the child not to make a section 117 application.

Chapter 15

Adverse Possession

The doctrine of adverse possession represents a way in which an individual can gain *de facto* rights through long user of someone else's land.

The Statute of Limitations 1957 prevents tort actions being brought after a certain period of time. It also operates to prevent actions relating to land being brought after a certain period of time. If someone else has been in adverse possession of your land for a certain period of time, 12 years, after that period has elapsed then your right to sue them and your consequent right to the land is extinguished. This gives that individual *de facto* rights. The person with the legal and equitable right to the land can no longer sue them. So long as they remain in possession their possession gives them a better title to the property than anybody else.

In order to decide whether adverse possession is present it must be shown that someone other than the landowner has been in possession of land for 12 years and that, throughout those 12 years, such possession was adverse to the landowner's rights.

The policy factors in favour of extinguishment of title by adverse possession are as follows: the doctrine encourages speedy recourse to legal actions, the quieting of title and the economic use of land. It avoids the problems attracted by unadministered estates. The doctrine of adverse possession was first introduced in the Real Property Limitation Act 1833 and is now contained in the Statute of Limitations 1957.

Four conditions must be satisfied in order for adverse possession to occur.

Throughout the period in question:

1. The individual whose title is alleged to be extinguished must have had a right to possession of the land.

2. The individual whose title is alleged to be extinguished must not have been in possession of the land.

3. Another individual (a squatter) must have been in possession of the land.

4. The possession of the squatter must have been adverse to that of the true owner. In other words, the squatter must have had what is known as an *animus possidendi*.

These conditions will be discussed in more detail below. A detailed knowledge of them will be required in the examination.

I: RIGHTS ACQUIRED BY THE SQUATTER UNDER THE DOCTRINE OF ADVERSE POSSESSION

It is important to note that the doctrine of adverse possession does not transfer any legal or equitable interest in the land to the squatter. In the nineteenth century, a different view was taken, and it was thought that adverse possession operated to convey of the title of the dispossessed owner to the squatter at the end of the relevant period. The Irish case of *Rankin v. McMurtry* ((1889) 24 L.R. Ir. 290) supported the parliamentary conveyance theory but this was rejected in *Tichborne v. Weir* ((1892) 67 L.T. 735; [1891-94]) and *O'Connor v. Foley* ([1906] 1 I.R. 20). It was agreed by the Supreme Court in *Perry v. Woodfarm Homes Ltd* ([1975] I.R. 104) that the parliamentary conveyance theory was no longer valid and that adverse possession only operated to extinguish the rights of the dispossessed owner. It did not transfer any *de jure* rights to the squatter.

However, so long as the squatter remains in possession of the relevant land he has *de facto* rights over the property. By virtue of his possession he has a claim over the land which is better than everyone except a person who can prove a legal or equitable title. This right, stemming from possession, is known as the *jus possidendi*. If the only person who can prove a legal or equitable title is the person whose rights have been extinguished, then there is no one who can oust the squatter so long as he remains in possession of the land.

For that reason, the rejection of the parliamentary conveyance theory does not pose much of a problem for squatters on freehold land. However, when the land adversely possessed is leasehold land, the rejection of the parliamentary conveyance theory has serious implications for the squatter, as will be seen below.

It should also be pointed out that a parliamentary conveyance may actually occur in favour of the squatter on registered land, where the terms of the Registration of Title Act 1964 allow the dispossessed person's interest in the land to be transferred to the squatter after 12 years' adverse possession.

However, in relation to unregistered leasehold land, it is very important to remember that adverse possession operates by extinguishing the title of the dispossessed owner, not by transferring it to the squatter.

II: REQUIREMENTS FOR ADVERSE POSSESSION

When is adverse possession present? It is important to remember that all the conditions below have to be present throughout a 12-year period.

1. The individual against whom the doctrine is being invoked must have had a present right to possession of the land in question during the period when adverse possession was alleged. Otherwise time does not run against him

For example, a landlord has no right to possession of land during the period of the lease. Therefore, if a squatter dispossesses a lessee, he extinguishes the lessee's title, but time does not run against the landlord until the lease terminates. Similarly, if someone has a vested or contingent future interest in the land, time does not run against them until that interest falls into possession. However, once time starts to run against such a party, he will have to act quickly since, as will be seen later, he is subject to a shorter limitation period.

2. The individual against whom the doctrine is being invoked must not have been in possession of that land during the relevant period

Sometimes it is difficult to decide if someone has gone out of possession of land or not. This is particularly true if the land is only used by them for a particular purpose and the need for that purpose did not occur at all during the period alleged. Can such a person be said to have gone out of occupation just because he or she did not go near the land during that time?

This was the argument raised in *Dundalk UDC v. Conway* (unreported, High Court, December 15, 1987). Here an area of land sloped down to a river. This area was only used by its owner when it was necessary to repair a bridge over the river. It was held that just because the owner had not gone near the land for 12 years and had not objected to his neighbour grazing cattle on it did not mean he had gone out of possession.

One possible way in such a situation to dispossess an owner who does not go near his land is for the squatter to put up a fence and lock it.

3. Someone else is in possession of the land

Such a person is usually known as a "squatter". In order for someone to qualify as a squatter, his acts over the land in question must amount to acts of possession. Merely playing on the land, keeping ponies there, walking and shooting are not normally equivalent to acts of possession. Acts which fall short of acts of possession may found a prescription claim and gain that person an easement after the relevant prescription period.

4. The possession by the squatter must be adverse to the other party's right to possession

There must be an *animus possidendi* on the part of the squatter, *i.e.* an intention to possess the land to the exclusion of all others, even the true owner.

A belief by the squatter that he is the true owner of the land will constitute a sufficient *animus possidendi*.

This is demonstrated by the case of *Murphy v. Murphy* ([1980] I.R. 183). Here a testator's widow had been entitled to his land by a residue clause in his will. She was not aware of this and treated the land as vested in her two sons. After the younger son sold his share, the other worked the land. The mother's title was held to have been extinguished by adverse possession on the part of the son.

Courts are particularly reluctant to find an *animus possidendi* on the part of the squatter in cases where the owner had no present use for the land, but intended to make use of it in the future, and the squatter's use of the land is not inconsistent with the owner's intended future use.

Leigh v. Jack ((1879) 5 L.R. Ex. D. 264) is a case demonstrating this point. Land was acquired for the purpose of making a street on it in the future. It was intended to lay idle in the meantime. The defendant used the land to store scrap metal. It was held that the plaintiff had not been dispossessed/had not discontinued possession. It was also held that there was no *animus possidendi* on the part of the defendant. He knew that the land was intended for future use, and his use was not inconsistent with that future use.

An Irish equivalent was *Cork Corporation v. Lynch* ([1995] 2 I.L.R.M. 598). A plot of land had been acquired by the plaintiffs with the intention that it should be used as part of a road development. The defendant owned a neighbouring garage and started to park cars on the plaintiff's land. He fenced around the plot and resurfaced it. However, there was held to be no *animus possidendi*. His occupation was not inconsistent with an intention of the local authority to use the land for road widening.

However, in *Durack (Seamus) Manufacturing v. Considine* ([1987] I.R. 677) the plaintiff's predecessors in title had purchased two fields to build a factory. Only one of the fields housed the factory. The defendant began to graze cattle in the unoccupied field and fenced around it. It was argued that the defendant's possession was not adverse because it was not inconsistent with the purpose for which the owner intended to use the land. The judge held that this point only went to negative an *animus possidendi* when there was actual knowledge by the squatter of the owner's future intentions in relation to the land:

> "An awareness of the landowner's intention was a factor which might make it reasonable to infer that there was no animus possidendi ... the intention of the landowner had no other relevance to the issue of whether there had been adverse possession".

Adverse possession can also be negatived if possession is with the authority of the owner, for example, if he can show that he had granted a licence or a lease to the squatter. But if a licence or lease has been granted and it comes to an end, there may be adverse possession after that date. If rent continues to be paid after the expiry of a fixed term lease, there will be an implied periodic tenancy and obviously no adverse possession. However, if rent is not paid there will be either a tenancy at will or a tenancy at sufferance. A tenancy at will will occur if the landlord expressly or impliedly consents to the tenant staying on. A tenancy at sufferance will arise if the landlord neither consents nor objects to the tenant staying on. Under the Statute of Limitations a tenant at sufferance is always in adverse possession against the landlord. After one year of a tenancy at will, the tenant at will begins to be in adverse possession.

The recent High Court case of *Griffin v. Bleithin* ([1999] 2 I.L.R.M. 182) demonstrates a liberal approach to the issue of *animus possidendi*. In this case the defendant alleged that he had a *de facto* right to a shed and part of a yard under the doctrine of adverse possession. The defendant had been granted the yard and shed under a weekly tenancy agreement in 1968. Notice to quit was served in 1974, terminating the tenancy. The tenant failed to leave, despite repeated requests from the owner. Quirke J. found that there had been adverse possession. The defendant had been in unlawful occupation of the premises since 1974. It was argued that the acts of the defendant were insufficient to show an *animus possidendi*, on the ground that the defendant had been absent from the yard and shed for significant periods, and also that the acts of user by the defendant, such as using the yard for parking vehicles and the shed for storing materials, might have been merely intended to assert an easement rather than a right to possession. These arguments were rejected by Quirke J.

III: SPECIAL SITUATIONS OF ADVERSE POSSESSION

Cumulative acts of adverse possession by a number of squatters can together serve to extinguish a title, *e.g.* if seven years' adverse possession by one squatter is followed immediately by five years' adverse possession by another. However, if there is a gap in time between the two periods of adverse possession, they cannot be added together to extinguish the owner's title.

In addition, time may stop running against the owner if there is a written and signed acknowledgment by squatter of the owner's rights, or if there have been payments from the squatter to the owner. If the owner is under a disability, such as infancy or insanity, time does not run against him during the period of disability. However, once the disability is over a squatter who has been in adverse possession for the requisite 12 years during the period of disability only has to show six years' adverse possession in order to extinguish the title.

If the squatter has obtained adverse possession by fraud, time does not run against the dispossessed owner until he knows of the fraud or could, with reasonable diligence, have discovered it.

IV: ADVERSE POSSESSION OF LEASEHOLD LAND

As regards adverse possession of land held on a lease or a tenancy, time does not normally start running against the lessor until the period of the lease is up. However, if rent is paid by the lessee to another person during that time time starts running against the lessor. The lessor's right to sue for rent is barred after six years, and his right to recover land by virtue of a forfeiture/breach of condition is barred 12 years after the breach occurs.

The rejection of the parliamentary conveyance theory has greatest significance in the context of adverse possession of leasehold land. As is known, time does not begin to run against the landlord until the tenancy comes to an end, unless the rent is paid to someone else. Twelve years should extinguish the right of the tenant. However, the problem is that the tenant's rights are not conveyed to the adverse possessor. For example, he has no right to see the lease and the landlord is under no obligation to accept rent from him. So it should not be difficult for the landlord to effect a forfeiture and put the original tenant back in place of the adverse possessor.

The rejection of the parliamentary conveyance theory also creates problems for the dispossessed tenant who is still liable to be sued on the covenants in his lease, although he has no way of observing them.

Thus, in the case of adverse possession of leaseholds, the squatter can be removed by a forfeiture on the part of the landlord, even if he is prepared to pay the rent and observe the covenants in the lease. This turns the whole principle of adverse possession on its head.

In the United Kingdom, the position goes even further against the squatter. In *Fairweather v. St.Marylebone Property Co. Ltd.* ([1963] A.C. 510) the House of Lords held that the dispossessed tenant, although he no longer had a right to sue the squatter, had a right under the lease which he could use to terminate the lease by surrender or merger. The word "extinguished" in the statute should be read as "extinguished against the squatter " rather than against the landlord.

This conclusion was reached on a very circuitous interpretation of the statutory provisions and was rejected by the Supreme Court in *Perry v. Woodfarm Homes Ltd.* ([1975] I.R. 104). However, the Supreme Court in *Perry* did recognise that although the squatter could not be got out by surrender or merger, he could be removed by a forfeiture. Henchy J. dissented and preferred the approach of the House of Lords in *Fairweather*. Griffin J.'s policy approach would appear to preclude forfeiture and sits uneasily with Walsh J.'s semantic analysis.

The present Irish position, therefore, is very far from the ideal, creating problems for both landlord and tenant. As Lord Denning points out in *Fairweather*, it is as easy for a landlord to organise a forfeiture as it is to organise a surrender or a merger. He merely has to refuse to accept rent from the squatter.

The problem does not exist in relation to registered land. This was recognised in the United Kingdom in the case of *Spectrum Investments Co. v. Holmes* ([1981] 1 W.L.R. 221) and by Walsh J. in *Perry*. This is because of the wording of the Registration of Title Act which allows the squatter to be registered as the owner of registered land after 12 years' adverse possession. Thus, a parliamentary conveyance may occur in relation to registered land.

The recent United Kingdom decision of *Central London Commercial Estates Ltd. v. Kato Kagaku Co. Ltd.* ([1998] 4 All E.R. 948) has resurrected, in that jurisdiction, the question of squatters' rights over leasehold land. This involved a situation where a squatter had dispossessed a tenant of registered land. Under *Spectrum Investments v. Holmes*, all that remained was for the squatter to register his title in order to be protected against a surrender, merger or forfeiture on the part of the landlord. However, the defendant in the case was somewhat tardy about registering his title. Before he had done so, the landlord arranged for the dispossessed tenant to surrender his interest to him and attempted to get the defendant out under *Fairweather*.

It was argued that *Spectrum Investments* was inapplicable because the squatter in that case had actually registered his title. However, the House of Lords rejected this view and refused to allow the surrender to take place. They identified a little known provision, section 75(1) of the Land Registration Act 1925. This stated that when a squatter had been in adverse possession of registered land for 12 years, the estate of the person he had dispossessed was to be held by that person on trust for the squatter, until such time as the squatter should register his title. The effect of this provision was that the dispossessed tenant held the leasehold estate on trust for the squatter. When the dispossessed tenant surrendered his interest to the landlord, the trusteeship passed with it. The landlord was compelled to treat the squatter as the equitable leasehold owner of the land, irrespective of whether the squatter had registered his title. Therefore he could not throw him off the land.

Were a similar situation to occur in Ireland, a different result would probably be reached, since the Registration of Title Act 1964 contains no equivalent of section 75(1). In Ireland a squatter on leasehold land would have to register his interest in order to protect himself from forfeiture. However, *Kato Kagaku* has certainly re-opened the debate

on squatters' rights in the United Kingdom, and perhaps the conclusion reached by the House of Lords in that case could be read as
indicating some dissatisfaction with *Fairweather*.

Index

143